The
WORTHLESS IRA

HOW TO KEEP WALL STREET
AND UNCLE SAM
FROM GETTING THEIR
GREEDY LITTLE FINGERS
ON YOUR HARD-EARNED MONEY

Joan,
Best Wishes in
your Retirement!

[signature]

JEFF BRUMMETT

THE WORTHLESS IRA

HOW TO KEEP WALL STREET AND UNCLE SAM FROM GETTING THEIR GREEDY LITTLE FINGERS ON YOUR HARD-EARNED MONEY

ISBN-10: 1-946203-33-5

ISBN-13: 978-1-946203-33-5

Expert Press

www.ExpertPress.net

Table of Contents

A Special Note of Thanks

I want to thank my parents for their undying love, support, and patience with me during all of life's ups and downs. Mom and Dad.... while we are all broken and imperfect vessels, your faithfulness and love for me throughout my life has shown me the face of God more clearly than you will ever know.

Special Notice of Disclaimer to Reader

This book is not intended to offer any advice on tax or investment strategy, nor is it intended to suggest any personal recommendation as to what may or may not be appropriate for any given individual to choose with regard to the most appropriate financial product or strategy available in the general market place today. Every individual's circumstance will differ and each person's situation therefore will be unique to the individual's wants, needs, priorities as dictated by life's circumstances. I strongly encourage the reader to seek professional advice from an experienced, knowledgeable, and licensed advisor who can offer current product options and can clearly explain their features and benefits as well as their limitations effectively. Each reader should vigorously pursue a strategy that they feel is uniquely best suited to meet their individual need and interest. The intent of this book is to help provoke readers to think through various retirement income realities and obstacles, and to help place a conservative value and perspective upon the various life insurance and annuity strategies discussed in the book. It is my goal that you will find this book a fascinating journey through a provocative look at our conventional wisdom's accepted financial and retirement planning system.

Part I

Understanding Financial Market History:
How We Got Here

Chapter One.

The Problem Is: Math is Math!

As we begin, lest my good friends on Wall Street accuse me of offering advice on the buying or selling of any financial instrument, let me offer this rather clear disclaimer:

I am not, do not, and will not <u>ever</u> offer advice on any securities product in this book. Period. Nothing in this book should be construed as said advice. I have no license to practice, nor offer advice, nor otherwise recommend in any way, shape, or form, to any person whatsoever, how, why, or when to buy or sell <u>any</u> securities-related product, instrument, or securities-related investment strategy.

Moreover, you would be a fool for taking such advice even if I did! I have no idea what the financial markets (or the people who may manipulate them) are going to do at any given point in time. Period.

The reader should also be aware that I do recommend, represent, and am licensed to advise and sell financial products and strategies commonly referred to as guaranteed safe money insurance contracts (a variety of annuities and various life insurance policies), which are backed solely by the claims paying ability of the life insurance companies.

Now that we've made that clear, let's have a candid conversation about the simple laws of mathematics. Specifically: How do these mathematical laws affect the performance of the financial strategies that are commonly leveraged today to help millions of Americans prepare for and navigate through the golden years of retirement? As they say, "The math is the math!"

I hated math in school. Where math is concerned, I'm nothing like my wife. How much does my wife love math? Well, while she was pursuing a dual Master's Degree at Indiana University in the IT field (I am so proud of you, sweetheart!), she would enthusiastically pay extra tuition and take high-level summer math classes—just for fun! All the other students were shouting for joy as they departed campus to enjoy their summer semester break. (Surely you've all done that at least once.) She was shouting for joy over math!

Okay, maybe I should clarify just a bit. I don't really *hate* math. I just never liked to spend *any* of my free time solving complex math problems solely for purpose of entertainment! As far as my wife and I are concerned, I guess it proves the old saying: "Opposites attract."

On the other hand, practical math ... *that* I have learned to love! Why? Because practical math—and the lifelong benefit it delivers—really is hard to beat. This is especially true when it comes to understanding how money, finance, interest yields, equity gains, equity losses, and retirement income strategies actually work in the real world.

We're going to talk a lot about the *real world* in this book. In the *real world*, there are only two types of people who retire:

1. Those who retire with more money in their nest egg than any rational, sane person could spend in a lifetime.

2. Those whose primary concern is how they manage *to not outlive* their nest egg. (Generally because these individuals *don't* have more money than a rational, sane person could spend in a lifetime!)

The question each of us must honestly answer is, "Which type of retiree am I?"

If we are honest with ourselves, the vast majority of us will fall into the second group of retirees. We may not identify as "have-nots," but our great-grandfather wasn't John D. Rockefeller. Nor are our children or grandchildren set for life, able to live off the money we'll leave behind. Instead, we work every day for most of our lives. To what end? Only to wake up each morning of retirement and be driven to our knees in prayer: "Lord, let this not be the day the financial markets decide to plummet and enter another prolonged retreat, as in the decade-long period of 2000–2010!" And why do we pray this fervent prayer? We simply **don't have** the kind of multigenerational wealth that would allow us to realize our retirement dreams while weathering another decade of negative asset growth. Especially now that our stage of life requires us to draw an income down against those financial assets!

The Paradigm Shift of Retirement Income Planning

How can you successfully transition from working years to retirement years? Without question, the most difficult aspect of the transition is *mental*. Every retiree who longs for a secure and successful retirement must face and overcome this mindset transition. What is the transition? It is the transition from an *accumulation-phase mindset* to a *distribution-phase mindset*. Why is this transition so necessary? It's simple, really. **The mathematical rules for survival and success during the *distribution* phase of our financial life (the retirement years) are completely _opposite_ of the rules that apply to the *accumulation* phase (our working years)**. As we move into and through our distribution years, not understanding the impact of these mathematical rules multiplies our risk of enormous peril and failure during retirement.

History is replete with individuals who enjoyed above-average success during their accumulation years, but ended up barely scraping by at some point during their *distribution* years. Or worse, they went broke and became dependent upon the generosity of family, friends, and church. Often because they simply didn't understand the impact of the mathematical rules that govern the distribution years of our financial life. Nearly all of us could tell the story of one such unfortunate soul.

The Promise versus Plight of Retirees Today

We live in the wealthiest nation on the planet. Despite this, the greatest fear of most U.S. citizens approaching retirement is whether they'll have the income they need during their retirement years. Recently, three thousand baby boomers were asked which they feared more: (1) death or (2) running out of money before death. Two thirds chose the latter.[1] To put it bluntly, retirees fear their money will die before they do! This is the great American retirement tragedy.

It was not supposed to be this way. This was not the picture painted by members of Congress and our elite friends on Wall Street. During the mid to late 1970s, these two dubious bedfellows united to rewrite our nation's tax laws. The result was the creation of the vaunted tax-deferred retirement savings programs known popularly today as the 401k and IRA. They told us their changes were "for the better." Nearly forty years later, this remains their story—in spite of the overwhelming and devastating statistics which portend otherwise. (A deep dive examination into the actual laws and rules that govern these lopsided financial monstrosities will be offered in chapters nine and ten).

Baby boomers retiring today probably remember the "three-legged stool" of retirement. This strategy was once touted as the ideal retirement model. It consisted of Social Security, defined benefit pensions, and personal savings. Tax-deferred savings programs, such as the 401k, were supposed to take the third leg (personal savings) and place it on steroids. The promise was that these new tax-deferred savings plans would cause an explosion of "supercharged growth" in personal savings, an explosion much like one would expect after throwing gasoline on an open flame.

In reality, none of the legs of the three-legged stool turned out to remotely resemble the promised picture of success. Today, the vast majority of retirees find themselves with barely a two-legged stool. Why? Because of an apparent "unintended consequence": the 401k has essentially killed the corporate pension.

Oops!

---

1 Walter Updegrave, "Here's What People Fear Most About Retirement — and How You Can Overcome It," accessed May 15, 2018 at http://time.com/money/4984420/retirement-fear-running-out-money/.

According to the Bureau of Labor Statistics, just 18 percent of private sector workers have a defined benefit pension today. This means that four-fifths of Americans have lost a primary source of guaranteed lifetime income.[2] To compound the worries of those retiring today, the Social Security trust fund is expected to deplete its reserves by 2034, and will only be able to fund approximately 75 percent of benefits after that.[3]

Translation: The benchmark leg of the three-legged retirement stool, Social Security, is severely cracked and rotting from the inside out. One might not want to lean too heavily upon that leg!

The math indicates that Social Security is in a dire, unsustainable, downward death spiral. The corporate pension is now gone for over 80% of private workers. Aren't you glad Congress and Wall Street poured gasoline on and fed steroids to the third "personal savings" leg of our retirement stool by creating a perpetual **risk-based, peril-filled savings plan**, the "tax-qualified savings plan" of the vaunted IRA/401k?

Yeah, right. Me too!

You're the Lucky One!

If you're reading this book, then you are one of the lucky ones. You managed to get through your accumulation years with enough savings to make reading this book worth your time. Congratulations! Whether you realize it or not, you are in the minority. According to an article posted on Investopedia, research by the **Insured Retirement Institute** found that fully 24% of Baby Boomers have *no retirement savings at all*—the lowest number since the study started in 2011. Even more troubling, only 55% of Baby Boomers have *some* retirement savings. And of those, 42% have less than $100,000.[4]

---

2   Economic Policy Institute, "Private-Sector Pension Coverage Fell by Half over Two Decades," January 11, 2013. Accessed May 15, 2018 at http://www.epi.org/blog/private-sector-pension-coverage-decline/.

3   U.S. Department of the Treasury, "Fact Sheet: Social Security and Medicare Trustees Report," July 22, 2015. Accessed May 15, 2018 at http://www.treasury.gov/press-center/press-releases/Pages/jl0127.aspx.

4   Barbara A. Friedberg, "Are We in a Baby Boomer Retirement Crisis?," June 7, 2017. Accessed May 15, 2018 at https://www.investopedia.com/articles/personal-finance/032216/are-we-baby-boomer-retirement-crisis.asp

According to the Economic Policy Institute, the median savings for boomers ages 56–61 in 2013 was a meager $163,577.[5] How can that level of savings be stretched into income for 30 years or more? (Better to plan for living and die sooner, than to plan for dying and live longer, right?) If one adheres to Wall Street financial planning's conventional wisdom, a 4% withdrawal is the maximum one should take. At a withdrawal rate of 4%, the average income from savings of $163,577 would be no more than $6,543 per year.

Another oops.

So what happened to the "steroid effect" of the tax-deferred personal savings plan? Math, in the form of Wall Street risk and fees—that's what happened!

The True Cost (Math) of Wall Street Fees

According to an article on the widely-respected financial website *The Motley Fool,*

> *the fees we pay for the retirement plans are surprisingly high. Moreover, the "Rebalance IRA Survey" found that about a fifth of full-time employed Americans, aged 50 to 68, think they pay less than 0.5% annually, and only 4% think fees top 2%. In fact, per the latest edition of the 401(k) Averages Book, the average fees deducted were 1.5% annually from workers' 401(k) accounts. Among smaller plans, some fees approached 2.5%, with at least one approaching 4%.[6]*

5   Monique Morrissey, "The State of American Retirement," March 3, 2016. Accessed May 15, 2018 at http://www.epi.org/publication/retirement-in-america/.

6   Selena Maranjian, "Understanding Retirement Plan Fees and Expenses Can Supercharge Your Savings," December 2, 2014. Accessed May 15, 2018 at https://www.fool.com/retirement/general/2014/12/02/understanding-retirement-plan-fees-and-expenses-ca.aspx.

Studies have shown that an average fee of only 1% can cost up to $590,000 in a relatively modest 401k investment savings program with contributions of only $10,000 per year.[7] Fees are a huge problem for savers—but a huge boom for advisers. Wall Street Financial Advisers hate the idea of clients trading in their equities-based investment portfolio for a *guaranteed lifetime income annuity product* at retirement. "Principal-protected annuities are terrible!"—so they say. Maybe that's because the Adviser would lose *his* lifetime "annuity": the income from yearly fees on his client's portfolio (regardless of how the portfolio performs).

The True Cost (Math) of Wall Street Risk

Fees aren't the only problem. Risk is a huge problem that Wall Street has managed to conceal from the minds of most everyday retirement investors. How much of a problem has the risk of loss caused in the retirement plans of those of us in the *Underclass* today?

A decade of backward earnings—going nowhere, slowly—not only destroyed the dreams of those who had just retired in 2000, but also rendered virtually impossible the dreams of those planning to retire anytime in the two decades to follow! Why? Because a decade of lost compound growth is a lost opportunity that compounds forever. In other words, Wall Street fees *never* stop costing you money, and neither do the losses! You never recover from a loss. Never! The lost opportunity costs of Wall Street fees and losses live and compound eternally.

Against all odds, while retired Americans struggle to make ends meet, the only class of Americans who are truly better off today are those who architected the current state of affairs back in the late seventies and early eighties: Wall Street and Congress. Yet somehow, remarkably, we've all been conditioned to

---

7   Dayana Yochim and Jonathan Todd, "How a 1% Fee Could Cost Millennials $590,000 in Retirement Savings." Accessed May 15, 2018 at https://www.nerdwallet.com/blog/investing/millennial-retirement-fees-one-percent-half-million-savings-impact/.

trust *their* "genius retirement system." We've been trained to follow the advice of *their* well-dressed, well-compensated army of financial advisers. We are expected to unquestioningly toe the line they draw for us, from cradle to grave.

This book is about challenging that system – philosophically, logically and mathematically.

You shouldn't read this book if you're looking to confirm what your Wall Street broker and financial adviser have told you. This book reveals the naked financial truth of our failed American retirement system. It's about all the things Wall Street and Uncle Sam don't want you to know. This book identifies what they absolutely don't want you to ever think about—let alone plan against – the Perils of real math during our distribution years!

For some, it may already be too late. I truly hope it's not too late for you. This book will demonstrate that every IRA and 401k is a ticking time bomb, potentially Worth*less*. What all of us have been led to believe about the underlying foundation of any IRA account is that the value of the stock prices and the overall market value contained within that account—are based upon things like corporate profits, positive balance sheets, earnings per share, price per share, and the like. Well, the problem is, this foundation is not what you and I have been led to believe. These things have far less to do with the actual underlying value than Wall Street would like us to believe. This book will prove that beyond a reasonable doubt, because math is math!

Have you sensed for quite some time that financial truth has been obfuscated, altered, and perverted in order to benefit the financial and political elite, at the expense of those of us in the *Underclass*? This book is written for you.

Let me be perfectly clear. **You will not learn how to become wealthy during retirement as a result of reading this book.** However, you will learn how to **preserve and *enjoy*** all that you have spent a lifetime acquiring. That money is *your* money. You should be the one to whom it brings joy, happiness and peace of mind. This book is for all those who agree with the words of that great sage Will Rogers:

"It's not the return **on my money** that concerns me at this point in life. It's the return **of my money** that worries me most!"

Let's begin by looking at a real-world retirement case study. One where the *impossible* proved to be *possible*. Because math is math! Isn't it?

Chapter Two.

"Average" Portfolio Returns: When Is 1.79% Greater Than 5.36%?

The successful management of money is highly dependent upon the realities of basic mathematics. After all, it's important to understand that $1 + $3 = $4. It's equally important to understand that $3–$4 = a $35 non-sufficient funds fee from your bank! And, of course, negative $1.

According to Max Tegmark, one of the world's leading theoretical physicists, math is what makes everything work—or break down. Without solid, reliable math, nothing could exist. At least that's what physicists like Tegmark tell us about the mathematically-based universe in which we all live.[8]

Since most retirees today have the vast majority of their savings invested in an array of stocks, bonds, and mutual funds, let's apply basic math principles to the rise and fall of the stock market. How might basic math affect our ability to make sound decisions as we prepare for and *live through* our retirement years? This should be fun!

Before we get too far into the thick of things, I want to make a promise to you. In this chapter we are going to learn two basic lessons:

---

8   Max Tegmark, "Everything in the Universe Is Made of Math – Including You," November 4, 2013. Accessed May 15, 2018 at http://discovermagazine.com/2013/dec/13-math-made-flesh.

1. How math affects our investment portfolio returns

2. How math and "sequence of returns" combine to profoundly affect the value of an investment portfolio—particularly during the *distribution* phase of retirement

To illustrate how math affects an investment portfolio's return, here is the fictitious story of a 65-year-old who is just about to retire. Let's call him Larry. Since this chapter is also about understanding history and historic context, we'll place Larry in the last week of December 1999.

❦

Larry had been a hard worker his entire life. He and his wife Diane raised two children, both young men who graduated from college several years ago. Larry and Diane made it! True empty nesters now, both were anticipating the golden years of retirement that lie straight ahead. After years of blood, sweat, and sacrifice, these coming years were to be *their years!*

Larry and Diane were debt free, owing absolutely nothing to anyone. This was certainly no surprise to those who knew them: Larry and Diane had been staunch savers their whole lives. When they bought a new car, it was always driven until it practically wouldn't start anymore. No one was going to tempt either of them to keep a shiny new Mercedes in the drive just to keep up appearances with the neighbors. It wasn't that Larry and Diane were cheap—far from it. They always had nice cars. Those cars just weren't Mercedes, nor were they shiny and new. Well, okay … shiny perhaps. Just not new.

It was the same with things like taking vacations and eating out. No one ever starved. Larry and Diane took the whole family on at least two week-long vacations every year. But they never stayed at the Ritz-Carlton or dined at Ruth's Chris Steakhouse.

All this modesty in lifestyle paid off. At age 65, Larry had accumulated that magical $1,000,000 in his 401k retirement portfolio. He had meticulously followed his investment adviser's advice over the years, and boy had it paid off! Larry was about to retire a millionaire. And unlike his two sons, Larry would do it without the benefit of a college degree! That's something he had every right to feel proud of. Larry had become a millionaire the old-fashioned way: years of sacrifice, loyalty, and hard work.

The big day was nearing, and Larry thought it best to schedule an appointment with Gordon, his trusted financial adviser of twenty years. Over the years, Larry had come to think of Gordon as more than just a trusted adviser. Gordon was a friend. Gordon and his wife Susan had taken Larry and Diane out for dinner one year as a client appreciation gesture, and that had been the beginning of a long friendship. Later on, Larry and Diane invited Gordon and his wife to attend church during a difficult period of life: Gordon lost his father, who passed at the relatively young age of 62. It was a hard time for Gordon, and the two couples grew a close friendship. Larry liked, admired, and trusted Gordon. Gordon felt the same way toward Larry. They were friends.

On the day of the big meeting Larry entered Gordon's office, sat down, and said, "Gordon, I think I'm ready to take the plunge into retirement. I just need to confirm with you that I've accumulated what Diane and I will need in order to sustain the lifestyle and income levels we will need as we move through our retirement years."

"Larry," Gordon said, "I'm happy to hear this for you and Diane. Of course I'm happy to review your plan and give you my best professional advice, as always."

"I'm counting on it," Larry replied with a humble and respectful tone. "Here's what we're thinking…."

Larry opened all of his portfolio statements and confirmed with Gordon that he and Diane had accumulated $1,000,000 down to the penny. Larry asked how much Gordon thought he and Diane could realistically take as a withdrawal against his IRA account balance without the risk of running out of money before both he and Diane had passed away.

Gordon laughed and told Larry he wished he had a nickel for every time a client asked him that question. "It's not an exact science, you know. There are lot of variables we have to consider—not the least of which is how long you and Diane decide to live! I will promise you this," he said with a smile, "the earlier you'll commit to dying, the more income per year I can give you!"

They both laughed, just how you would expect good friends to laugh together. That's one thing Larry really liked about Gordon. He had a great sense of humor and always made Larry feel at ease when they talked about serious matters like this.

"Well, I can tell you that Diane is promising to spoil our grandkids well into the third generation," Larry replied. "So give me something that errs on the side of longevity, just in case she ends up making good on that promise."

Again, the two friends laughed aloud. They both knew that Diane's love and passion for her grandchildren was legendary. "Fair enough," Gordon said. "Let's see what we can do."

Gordon pulled some historical data on the performance of Larry's portfolio since its inception back in 1980. Larry had enjoyed the typical result of nearly all Gordon's clients. Gordon was one of the better financial advisers in the country. Over the years, his clients had many years where they were able to beat the benchmark growth of the S&P 500 — the gold standard of portfolio performance measurements within the financial world of managed money. The S&P 500 had a reputation for routinely besting more than 80% of managed portfolios over time. Not so with Larry's portfolio, though. Gordon was one of the really good advisers!

"Larry, we've worked hard together. You've earned an average growth of just over 18% per year for the last twenty years. This is just slightly more than a half percent better than what the S&P 500 has done over that same period of time. So we've done very well indeed. But to be honest, I don't want to promise that kind of performance over the next twenty years. When clients begin to consider their retirement years, I like to err on the side of caution and make conservative assumptions. After all, each of us has only one chance to get it right in retirement. There is no free 'do over' should we get it wrong. So let's discount your historic return rate by sixty percent, from an 18% return down to a 7% return. That ought to give us a conservative ballpark estimate upon which we can confidently rely. As for taking withdrawals, again, I would rather under promise and over deliver. So, let's knock an extra two points off our 7% conservative return assumption. This would put you in roughly a 5% draw down bracket. Will a 5% withdrawal get you where you need to be?"

Though Larry was not a college graduate, he had always been good at math. A quick calculation told him that 5% was sufficient to meet his and Diane's needs. He also appreciated Gordon's conservative approach, though quietly he hoped Gordon was not seriously thinking 7% would be the best he and Diane could achieve moving forward into the future. That just seemed a far cry from the 18% he'd been accustomed to averaging *over the last 20 years from 1980 through 2000!* Larry gazed quietly toward the floor's deep blue carpet for slightly more than a minute. Then, with a sober and solemn look in his eyes, Larry looked at his friend and raised his and Diane's most pressing concern.

"Gordon, I like the budget for withdrawals that you've proposed. But in a worst-case scenario, would it ever put us in jeopardy of depleting our nest egg before we both die? Should I be the first to go, I don't want Diane ever running out of income. She has never had to work—and I don't want her to be forced to start once I'm gone."

"Well, Larry, like I said, there are a lot of unknowns. No one knows for sure. Nevertheless, we've been at this a long time. Twenty years is not exactly a flash in the pan. Granted, there have been a few lean years, and your portfolio may not do as well moving forward. But to answer your question definitively, it's hard for me to imagine a scenario that would cut our returns by more than 60% moving forward in time. The conventional wisdom is that the U.S. economy continues to be driven by very strong underlying fundamentals. Even with a conservative rebalancing of your portfolio, you have to consider the fact that the market has averaged a return of more than 10% annually over the last century. That's a hundred years of data upon which to gauge your future. That should give you some peace of mind. Don't you agree?"

Larry did agree. Gordon was right. Surely the market would not underperform by more than 60% over the next 20–30 years. "So, Gordon, if Diane and I needed to take, oh, $50,000 a year, and index it with an annual cost-of-living adjustment (COLA) of 3% to account for inflation, you think we'd be okay?"

Gordon thought as he ran some quick numbers on his calculator. "Hmm…. Math is math, Larry. And a quick run of the math says you and Diane should be more than okay."

"How sure are you?"

"Honestly, Larry, even the most conservative projections espoused in our industry today—and endorsed by people a lot smarter than me—indicate that a 6% withdrawal rate should be a safe rule of thumb."

[Note: While a 6% withdrawal rate sounds ridiculously high by today's standard, nevertheless, 6% was the rule of thumb of conventional wisdom back in the 1990s. After all, why not? The market was approaching the end of a 20-year cycle where the average annual return of the S&P 500 with dividends reinvested was nearly triple 6% (17.4%, to be exact)—for 20 years!]

Gordon continued, "So if we're only drawing down at 5% after averaging 18% over the last 20 years, you and Diane should be golden!"

Larry was relieved. He knew Gordon would give him straight talk and solid financial advice. With renewed confidence, Larry felt ready to make wise decisions with Diane about how to enjoy their golden years. After hearing Gordon's thoughts, perspective, and professional advice, Larry finally permitted himself to feel a measure of excitement about the days and years that lay ahead. He reached across the desk and shook Gordon's hand: "Thank you for all your hard work, patience, support—and especially friendship—over the years. Let's make it happen." With a confident smile beginning to wash across his face, Larry asked, "Can we start this plan on Monday?"

"You bet we can," Gordon answered. "I'll take care of everything. All you have to do is go enjoy your retirement."

And that was that.

It was Christmas of 1999. Larry had just retired at the age of 65. He'd made it. The American dream was his. It was time for Larry and Diane to ride into the sunset and enjoy their golden years!

In truth, neither Gordon nor Larry could have had any idea what peril was hiding in the financial markets over the next 10 years.

However, with the benefit of hindsight, you and I do.

Larry would not average even the 60%-discounted return that Gordon suggested in his most conservative assumptions. Over the next 18 years, the S&P

500—the gold standard of market indices—would plummet to an annual net average return of only 5.36% (after Gordon's fee). Still, Larry was only targeting a 5% withdrawal rate with a modest COLA of 3% to account for inflationary erosion to his purchasing power. Surely a market that averaged even a miserable 5.36% net of fees would be sufficient for him and Diane to squeeze out 25 years of income. After all, at 0% growth their money would last 18 years, COLA adjustments and all. With a 5.36% average net annual return, squeezing out another seven or eight years couldn't be so difficult. Could it? Besides, Larry was only kidding with Gordon. Truthfully, neither he nor Diane expected to live past 85 years of age. Surely things would work out fine….

⁕

Although this story revolved around fictional characters, the scenario is more than pretend. In fact, millions of people had similar "fictional" conversations with their financial advisers back at the turn of the century. How do I know this? I hear their stories when they come to my retirement planning seminars or contact me through my weekly radio show. Believe me when I tell you that no client nor advisor in the financial planning world at the end of 1999 was remotely close to predicting what was about to happen in the financial markets over the next 10 years. Nobody!

[Contextual Note: From the Reagan years of the 80s through the Clinton years of the 90s, our nation's economy grew at a steady and consistent pace—with relatively modest and always short-lived setbacks. Our financial markets (think people's IRA and 401k accounts) had skyrocketed beyond anyone's expectations. Millionaires were being made in the middle class by the thousands, for the first time in history. You could find middle-class millionaires in almost every corner of the country: big cities, small cities, even tiny little towns. City dwellers and country folk were becoming millionaires with the advent of this newfangled 401k market investing thing … and, of course, with the help of trusted financial investment advisers like Gordon.]

Wall Street Projections ... Were Wrong

Let's take a look at Larry's portfolio to see exactly what did happen. When Larry retired at the end of 1999, the stock market had been on a 12-year bull market run, pressing against a new all-time high virtually every month for the past several years. In fact, during the 5 years prior to Larry's retirement, the S&P 500 had returned an average of 24% annually.[9] The economy was booming.

Optimism about America's future on Wall Street saturated financial-market prognosticators everywhere. One now rather *infamous* prognosticator, Robert Zaccaro, a Wall Street CFA, wrote a book predicting that the Dow would race to 30,000 by the year 2008![10] History, as they say, is always its own maker. Over the next decade, history refused to follow the optimism held by Wall Street. The results on retirees of that era were devastating. People like Larry saw their life savings decimated. Completely unbeknown to anyone on Wall Street, the opening decade of the new millennium was the most tumultuous and volatile period for the stock market since the inception of the IRA/401k stock market era. Larry's portfolio did not reach the conservative 7% Gordon had projected. Moreover, all three major indices—the S&P 500, the Dow 30, and the NAS-DAQ 100—produced **negative returns**! (This was true even with dividends reinvested.)

Wait a minute! That can't be right, can it? A decade of net negative returns? Surely a decade of negative returns was impossible. Wasn't it?

Actually, it was possible. It had even happened once before. When? During the period of time beginning in the year 1929 and lasting through 1939: the Great Depression!

Such would be the case once again, beginning in the year 2000. The advent of the new century brought on a decade of lost investment-savings opportunity. It threatened financial ruin for people like Larry and Diane—as well as virtually an entire generation of baby boomers marching behind them. Larry

---

9 DQYDJ, "S&P 500 Return Calculator, with Dividend Reinvestment," May 6, 2018. Accessed May 15, 2018 at https://dqydj.com/sp-500-return-calculator/.

10 Robert Zuccaro, *Dow to 30,000 by 2008: Why it's Different This Time*, Palisade Press (2003).

and Diane were forced to take withdrawals while investment accounts stayed underwater for 14 of the next 16 years. What should have been the best 16-year period of Larry and Diane's retirement life—utterly destroyed!

This was bad for Larry and Diane. And it was bad for millions of real people who retired during this time period. But even worse is the knowledge that *they all could have avoided this devastation.* How? By embracing the guaranteed income strategies recommended in chapters eleven through fifteen this book.

What if people who retired at the turn of the new century were given a second chance? If given a "do over," how many would opt for the promise of a guaranteed income? The first time these people chose a portfolio full of *risk* and a promise of merely *potential* gain. If given a second chance, might they choose differently next time around? Hindsight is always 20/20. Of course it is always better to not lose money, than to lose money! Larry and Diane are no exception.

Speaking of hindsight, let's look at what actually happened to Larry and Diane's retirement income account. The math behind their account will both surprise and enlighten all those who are about to follow Larry and Diane into their retirement years.

Remember that at the beginning of this chapter I promised you two lessons:

1. How math affects our investment portfolio returns

2. How math and "sequence of returns" combine to profoundly affect the value of an investment portfolio—particularly during the *distribution* phase of retirement.

We're about to learn the first lesson.

To help illustrate the math behind the numbers, I've created a simple chart for you to consider in a moment. As you follow the math in the chart, you'll be amazed at the outcome for Larry and Diane—and for their retirement dreams.

But before we look at the chart, let's have another fictional conversation with Larry and his trusted financial adviser Gordon. This time, let's pretend that Gordon actually has *supernatural predictive abilities.* We'll pretend that Gordon has a magic crystal ball that allows him to see into the financial future.

As we pick up the conversation, Larry has just asked Gordon what he thinks the market will do in the future.

❦

"Larry," Gordon began, "you are very fortunate to have me as your financial adviser. I happen to have special knowledge of the financial market's future. This is why your account has performed so well over the past twenty years! My crystal ball has revealed to me that there are only two possible places in which you can invest that will yield a positive return."

This definitely got Larry's attention. He looked up at Gordon, now with a significant measure of concern beginning to wash across his paling face.

"Really, Gordon? But how can that be, when things have gone so well over the last twenty years? Surely that's not possible!"

"Believe me, old friend," Gordon replied, "not only is it possible, it's worse than you think. You've been accustomed to average returns of 18% for the last twenty years—not to mention 24 percent over the last 5 years! Things are different in the future, my friend. Of the two investments which offer a positive return in the future, one will net an average of 5.36% after my fees. The other will net an average of 1.79% after fees. Larry, while I think I know the answer, I still have to ask the question. Which investment option would you prefer?"

Larry wasn't a college graduate like Gordon. Nevertheless, he was no idiot, and only an idiot would pick anything other than the 5.36% account!

"Put me in the 5.36% account," Larry said in a disheartened and disbelieving voice. He could gather only a little solace from Gordon's doomsaying: Even with a terrible return of 5.36%, his money should last until he and Diane were well into their 90s. Maybe longer, if they needed it to. "Surely that's sufficient," he reasoned quietly to himself.

But it wasn't sufficient. Not even close.

❦

Here's the first lesson about math. As the chart below illustrates, Larry and Diane were not able to take their full COLA-adjusted income withdrawals as they planned and budgeted. Instead, they ran out of money **just 14 years into their retirement**. See chart below:

Do the "Sequence" of Returns and "Fees" Matter Through Your Retirement Years?
(Or is it all just about getting the hightest "Average" Rate of Return?)

Historical Performance of the S&P 500 Index with Dividends Reinvested and Its Effect on Your Retirement Portfolio*
S&P 500 Index

*Source: https://ycharts.com/indicators/sandp_500_total_return_annual
Year End Withdrawal Includes **3% Per Year COLA Inflation Adjustment

Month	Year	Client Age	Account Value	One Year Index Return	Management Fee	Change In Value	Year End Withdrawal**	Year End Value
December	2000	65	$ 1,000,000	-9.10%	-1.50%	$ 894,000	$ (50,000)	$ 844,000
December	2001	66	$ 844,000	-11.89%	-1.50%	$ 730,988	$ (51,500)	$ 679,488
December	2002	67	$ 679,488	-22.10%	-1.50%	$ 519,129	$ (53,045)	$ 466,084
December	2003	68	$ 466,084	28.68%	-1.50%	$ 592,766	$ (54,636)	$ 538,129
December	2004	69	$ 538,129	10.88%	-1.50%	$ 588,606	$ (56,275)	$ 532,331
December	2005	70	$ 532,331	4.91%	-1.50%	$ 550,483	$ (57,964)	$ 492,519
December	2006	71	$ 492,519	15.79%	-1.50%	$ 562,900	$ (59,703)	$ 503,198
December	2007	72	$ 503,198	5.49%	-1.50%	$ 523,275	$ (61,494)	$ 461,782
December	2008	73	$ 461,782	-37.00%	-1.50%	$ 283,996	$ (63,339)	$ 220,657
December	2009	74	$ 220,657	26.46%	-1.50%	$ 275,733	$ (65,239)	$ 210,495
December	2010	75	$ 210,495	15.06%	-1.50%	$ 239,038	$ (67,196)	$ 171,842
December	2011	76	$ 171,842	2.11%	-1.50%	$ 172,890	$ (69,212)	$ 103,678
December	2012	77	$ 103,678	16.00%	-1.50%	$ 118,712	$ (71,288)	$ 47,424
December	2013	78	$ 47,424	32.39%	-1.50%	$ 62,073	$ (73,427)	$ -
December	2014	79	$ -	13.69%	-1.50%	$ -	$ (75,629)	$ -
December	2015	80	$ -	1.40%	-1.50%	$ -	$ (77,898)	$ -
December	2016	81	$ -	11.96%	-1.50%	$ -	$ (80,235)	$ -
December	2017	82	$ -	18.73%	-1.50%	$ -	$ (82,642)	$ -

Total Return = 123.46%   "Average" Annual Return (After Fees)
5.36%

Larry and Diane were about to learn a lesson no one had ever taught them. It would be an expensive lesson to learn at this point in their financial lives. That lesson? The often-irrevocable effect of something called "Sequence of Returns." (This will be the second lesson I promised you.)

Gordon correctly predicted that investing in the market would return an average of 5.36% over the next 18 years. However, the distribution phase of one's financial life is very different from the accumulation phase. Why is it so different? Unlike the accumulation years, once distributions begin, an unlucky **sequence of returns** can quickly destroy any future that a positive **average rate of return** seems to promise.

Such was the case for Larry and Diane. Negative returns during the first three years of their retirement drove Larry and Diane into a portfolio hole—a hole from which they were simply never able to climb out. Even though the subsequent years of 2004–2018 averaged a very respectable 9.6% return, by then it was too late. The damage had already been done in those early years. Larry and Diane went broke while still in the prime of their golden years, long before either had turned 80. In fact, Larry and Diane could not even draw out the full $1,000,000 they had spent a lifetime sacrificing to accumulate. Because of market losses and fees, they only withdraw a total income of $842,964 before going broke.

Are you surprised? I can assure you, Larry and Diane were.

The Math Logic Behind "Average" vs. "Real"

Allow me to walk you through a much simpler version of the relevant math that threatens all retirement investors. Suppose I have $100,000 invested in an account. In year one, my account loses 50%. Not good, but hey … I'm in this for the long haul, right?

Another year passes and now, at the end of year two, my account has delivered a net annual increase of 50%. What is my average rate of return for those two years? If you said zero, you know your math! Negative 50%, plus positive 50%, divided by 2 years, equals 0%! The math all works and sounds fine **until you put actual numbers into the equation**.

Follow me here…

- Year one: $100,000 x a negative 50% return = $50,000.

- Year two: $50,000 x a positive 50% return = $75,000.
  (Because $50,000 x 50% = $25,000; $25,000 + $50,000 = $75,000)

Herein lies the problem. If my actual return was 0%, one would rightly think I should still have $100,000 in my account. But I don't! I have $75,000… which is an *actual loss* of 25%! That's no small loss **while averaging a 0% return!**

Hear ye, hear ye! An "average" rate of return means absolutely nothing—especially during the *distribution* phase of one's financial life! The truth is, an "average rate of return" is Worth*less*, unless there is never a *negative* year in the *sequence* of those years. This is why any true retirement **income planner** will tell you that the primary concern when creating a plan for **retirement income** is the **elimination of negative returns during all years of distribution**. Even a *single* negative return during your retirement distribution years can potentially destroy the ability to ensure you don't outlive your money.

Think about it. Just. One. Big. Negative. Year. Is all it takes!

I'm about to ask you to consider a very serious question. Is it wise to assume such enormous risk during a period of life when your financial future is so utterly vulnerable to loss? If you were left without other alternatives, perhaps that would be one thing. But what if you didn't have to assume any market risk in order to guarantee success and a lifetime of reasonable growth and/or income? (Even income that could be guaranteed to increase over time!) Had Larry and Diane converted Larry's $1,000,000 401k to a guaranteed income annuity IRA:

1. Their principal would have never been lost.

2. Even if they had outlived their principal and growth, neither would have ever outlived the 3% COLA increasing annual income from the account. Never!

3. Had either of Larry or Diane ever needed Long Term Care, their COLA-adjusted income could have been doubled for up to five years.

4. All without any risk of ever running out of income—Ever!

With these tremendous guarantees and the accompanying peace of mind inevitably enjoyed from such guarantees, why would anyone opt for a risk of failure? Is it possible that we all choose risk because that's what the conventional system tells us to do—not because it makes good sense to do it? Who in their right-thinking mind would chose risk over guarantees where their financial future and retirement is concerned if they were not so strongly conditioned by *conventional* wisdom to do otherwise? No one! Rather, we are all conditioned to choose risk from cradle to grave. For whose benefit? This book will demonstrate beyond a reasonable doubt that we are conditioned by the *Wall Street system* for the **certain** benefit of Wall Street. Our assumption of risk is the **system's** guaranteed reward. Not ours. We have all been trained and conditioned to reward the system and those who control it. The only *guaranteed* reward for our assumption of risk exists only for those who sell it—RISK!

The Power of Sequence of Returns

Our risk of failure during retirement years multiplies greatly due to the factor of time now working against the risk taker, and due to sequence of returns.

Sequence of returns is the order in which returns materialize. Once an individual enters the distribution years of retirement, sequence of returns is even more important than *average rate of return*. Larry and Diane's average rate of return for the 18-year period from 2000 to 2017 was 5.36%. What if we double that to 11.52%? They could still go broke by the end of 2014! Why? Because of the *sequence* in those returns. You will see this clearly in a moment.

Here's the problem with sequence of returns. No one knows what the sequence of good years versus bad years will be. So, let me ask you a scary question. (Brace yourself!) What would happen if, in the first four years of your retirement, the market collapsed and lost 90% of its value?

I can already hear the defiant cry of the Wall Street financial adviser ... "But. That. Won't. Happen!"

Really?

Not only could it happen—it already has happened! This impossible disaster actually **struck once before during another period of time when investors on Wall Street "thought not, said not, and promised not."** That time period came at the end of the Roaring Twenties and upon the precipice of the Great Depression.

The era preceding the Great Depression was characterized by a sustained run of growth in the stock market—much like today. There are an uncanny number of parallels between the crash that ushered in the Great Depression and what many economic historians perceive in today's post-2008 bull market run.

In the year that led up to the Great Depression, by August of 1929, the Dow 30 had risen over 47% for the year. That is a tremendous start to the year by anyone's standard. To further embolden the confidence and euphoria of investors on Wall Street, this magnificent run up was preceded by a twelve-year-strong bull market averaging 18.6% returns annually with dividends reinvested over that same twelve year period of time. A twelve-year bull market is long enough to make investors forget that *nothing lasts forever!* Confidence in the new American economy post-World War 1 had never been higher. America had proven itself militarily invincible. Now America was proving itself economically invincible. Such was the sentiment of the day. Few dared sound the slightest warning over the massive margin of debt that bankers and investors had pumped into the financial markets in order to help produce this false run up of imaginary wealth. (Imaginary because debt *never* equals long term wealth.) The few brave souls who did pronounce warnings were shouted down as naysayers to the American spirit of optimism.

However, the future is always its own maker. It's just as the risk disclaimer proclaims: "past performance does not guarantee future results." History reminds us that tomorrow can turn for the worse in the blink of an eye. In fact, the speed of collapse is the very essence and nature of the term "economic *crash.*" From 1929 on, the market spent the next four years in a downward spiral, losing nearly 90% before it bottomed out.[11] All the way down, Wall Street advisers held their ground, telling investors, "Don't panic! It's only a paper loss. Hang in there, you're in this for the long haul!" Does this sound familiar?

---

11 DQYDJ, "S&P 500 Return Calculator, with Dividend Reinvestment," May 6, 2018. Accessed May 15, 2018 at https://dqydj.com/sp-500-return-calculator/.

Why Always the Long Way Home?

Virtually every major economic crash in history has occurred at a point in time when people thought not. And the recovery always takes longer than the collapse. This is true, in part, because the math behind a recovery is stacked against the investor. Recovery requires a higher percentage of return—and, subsequently, more time—than a loss does. A crash, by its very definition, happens quickly. After the crash that led to The Great Depression, it took fifteen years for the market to return to its previous 1929 high. Wall Street was right. The market did come back. Fifteen years later! Rebuilding from the effects of a crash always takes longer and costs more—these are time and costs one simply cannot afford during retirement years.

For example, when a 50% monetary loss is absorbed, a 100% gain is required to recover. Did you catch that? You need a 100% gain to cover a 50% loss! Which takes longer:

- a 50% market crash, or

- a 100% gain (doubling) of the market's value?

Retirees must understand this fundamental mathematical dynamic. Anticipating a 20–30 year retirement period, one should carefully consider which strategy is best suited to ensure surviving "the long haul."

Here's another scary question. Which is more devastating:

- 10 years of negative net cumulative returns?

- Or a 4-year decline of nearly 90%?

While both scenarios could obviously be devastating, is either scenario a realistic reason for concern? A Wall Street purveyor of risk might argue that these risks are neither realistic nor probable. However, **both scenarios have happened before**. Ask the people who retired at the beginning of 1929! These poor folks were the beneficiaries of a two-for-one, as the 4-year decline introduced the negative 10 year return. Strike one.

Fast forward and in the year 2000, a two-for-one also hit retirees who had a bulk of their 401k invested in the hot technology stocks of the NASDAQ. These poor unlucky souls encountered a 70% crash, and the market needed 14 years to climb back to the baseline set by the market in 2000. Strike two.

Approaching retirement, perhaps a true prudent and conservative investor should ask, "What *could* happen that *hasn't* happened yet?" Given what has already happened, this is quite the frightening question. Don't be strike three! Financial products that offer guarantees apart from market risk provide the peace of mind most retirees hope for during their retirement years.

Nevertheless, a Wall Street financial adviser never wants an investor to give serious thought to the possibility of the unthinkable. (Especially if that investor now possesses the largest nest egg of his life, which is the source of a Wall Street Broker's livelihood.) Yet a truly conservative, fiduciary, and defensive advisory approach toward retirement income planning **would mandate exactly such thinking**. Wouldn't it? The Book of Proverbs says,

"A sensible man watches for problems ahead and prepares to meet them. The simpleton never looks and suffers the consequences." Proverbs 27:12 TLB[12]

Simpletons rush straight into the myriad of global geopolitical and financial problems that undoubtedly lie ahead. And they suffer the consequences. Why not protect yourself financially against the un-happenable, the unthinkable, and the unrecoverable? Do we all not insure our home for such things? Is our retirement savings nest egg less important than our home? Would one even think about not insuring a home? Why would we not also want to "insure" our retirement nest egg? Some have a sense that unthinkable calamities are far more probable today than at any time in human history. Could events lurking in our financial market's future prove to be "unrecoverable"? Certainly we hope not. But honesty would force each of us to admit: we know not. Wisdom and subsequent peace of mind are likely to be found in a financial strategy that is *not* founded upon the principle of **risk, especially once time is no longer on our side.** As they say, "Discretion is the better part of valor." For prudent, conservative investors, retirement is not the time to abandon discretion and throw caution to the wind while risking it all.

---

12 Footnote accordingly.

Zero Can Be Your Hero in a Market Crash – Ask Larry!

Let's go back to the final question Gordon asked Larry in our second retirement income planning scenario. Do you remember it?

"Of the two investments which offer a positive return in the future, one will net an average of 5.36% after my fees. The other will net an average of 1.79% after fees. Larry, while I think I know the answer, I still have to ask the question. Which investment option would you prefer?"

What if, in a moment of utter insanity, Larry told Gordon to place him in the 1.79% investment? You're probably thinking, "No, no, no. There is no way that a 1.79% account could be in Larry and Diane's better interest."

Truth is sometimes stranger than fiction. Truthfully the 1.79% account could be superior … *if* **it never has a negative year.** Sequence of Returns combined with zero years of negative returns has incredible power. All retirees should have this powerful combination working on their behalf. It's like the proverbial "one-two punch" which knocks the potential of retirement failure out cold.

Prepare to witness the impossible: How a 1.79% **actual** annual return utterly destroyed a 5.67% **average** annual return. See the illustrative chart on the next page and compare it to the previous chart.

Amazing! With modest (never over 3.50%) yet *positive* returns each year, the lower average net return of 1.79% *destroyed* the 5.36% return option. The 5.36% "average" return is 66% higher. Nevertheless, Larry and Diane still ran out of money in 2013, as the previous chart showed. Yet the 1.79% "real" return carried Larry and Diane into their 82nd year with $29,792 dollars to spare!

Who among us would not have bet the farm **against** the 1.79% return?

During your distribution phase, chasing the *potential* of a higher "average" return while carrying a *risk* of negative returns is a fool's bet! Positioning yourself to achieve only positive (real) returns by avoiding all possible negative returns is the far more certain way to ensure a stress-free retirement **income strategy.**

Do the "Sequence" of Returns and "Fees" Matter Through Your Retirement Years?
(Or is it all just about getting the hightest "Average" Rate of Return?)

Month	Year	Client Age	Account Value	One Year Index Return	Management Fee	Change In Value	Year End Withdrawal*	Year End Value
December	2000	65	$1,000,000	3.07%	-1.50%	$ 1,015,700	$ (50,000)	$ 965,700
December	2001	66	$ 965,700	3.50%	-1.50%	$ 985,014	$ (51,500)	$ 933,514
December	2002	67	$ 933,514	3.50%	-1.50%	$ 952,184	$ (53,045)	$ 899,139
December	2003	68	$ 899,139	3.50%	-1.50%	$ 917,122	$ (54,636)	$ 862,486
December	2004	69	$ 862,486	3.50%	-1.50%	$ 879,735	$ (56,275)	$ 823,460
December	2005	70	$ 823,460	2.87%	-1.50%	$ 834,741	$ (57,964)	$ 776,778
December	2006	71	$ 776,778	3.50%	-1.50%	$ 792,313	$ (59,703)	$ 732,611
December	2007	72	$ 732,611	3.50%	-1.50%	$ 747,263	$ (61,494)	$ 685,769
December	2008	73	$ 685,769	3.49%	-1.50%	$ 699,416	$ (63,339)	$ 636,077
December	2009	74	$ 636,077	3.50%	-1.50%	$ 648,799	$ (65,239)	$ 583,560
December	2010	75	$ 583,560	3.50%	-1.50%	$ 595,232	$ (67,196)	$ 528,036
December	2011	76	$ 528,036	3.50%	-1.50%	$ 538,596	$ (69,212)	$ 469,385
December	2012	77	$ 469,385	3.50%	-1.50%	$ 478,772	$ (71,288)	$ 407,484
December	2013	78	$ 407,484	3.50%	-1.50%	$ 415,634	$ (73,427)	$ 342,207
December	2014	79	$ 342,207	3.50%	-1.50%	$ 349,052	$ (75,629)	$ 273,422
December	2015	80	$ 273,422	0.00%	-1.50%	$ 269,321	$ (77,898)	$ 191,422
December	2016	81	$ 191,422	1.00%	-1.50%	$ 190,465	$ (80,235)	$ 110,230
December	2017	82	$ 110,230	3.50%	-1.50%	$ 112,435	$ (82,642)	$ 29,792

Total Return: 55.93%

Average Annual Return (After Fees): 1.79%

Do you want to win in retirement?

Seriously! Do you want to **win with a stress-free, worry-free retirement income** for you and your spouse, regardless of how long either of you live?

Do you want to guarantee that the net savings of a life of hard work and sacrifice continue to provide financially for your surviving spouse long after you are gone?

If you want financial peace, start by eliminating risk on your net savings. Particularly, secure the portion of your savings necessary to guarantee the net *income* necessary in order to last until the day you and your spouse die.

Wall Street equity portfolio investing does not talk about a *guaranteed steady income* that lasts your *lifetime*. Why? Because this can only come from a financial product backed by the guarantees of a highly-rated life insurance company. Only a life insurance company will offer you a contract of **guaranteed lifetime income**. And Wall Street doesn't make money and can't charge fees when you choose a non-securities based investment strategy!

Here's a suggestion.

As you near (or enter) retirement, make a licensed and well-qualified life insurance agent a part of your financial planning team. He or she should specialize in retirement **IN-come** planning (in contrast to Wall Street **IF-come** planning). Ideally, you would start the relationship ten years before you retire. But as the saying goes, "Better late than never!"

Ready to continue our provocative education concerning the real history of our financial markets and how we got here? I hope so, because the retirement planning story is about to get even more interesting!

It's time to have some fun with a bit of *conspiratorial conjecture.* (Or not...?)

Chapter Three.

From Guarantees to Living in Peril While Relying on Risk: The Evolution of Retirement Planning

Wise men throughout history have proclaimed in order to make good decisions for the future, one must understand the past. As novelist George Santayana put it, "Those who cannot remember the past are condemned to repeat it."[13] We've all heard this. No one in their right mind argues against it. But do we follow it? All too often, we get in a hurry and fail to discipline ourselves to follow advice we know to be wise. Welcome to a dose of discipline!

To prepare for the most important financial days that lie ahead—your retirement—might it be wise to consider the history of our financial systems and the conventional retirement planning strategies we follow today? How were these systems engineered? Why were they created? In other words, from a financial retirement system strategic planning standpoint, how did we get "here"?

Today, "here" predominantly indicates a financial strategy that imperils and risks a substantial part of the average person's life savings until the very day

---

13 Wikiquote, "George Santayana." Accessed May 15, 2018 at https://en.wikiquote.org/wiki/George_Santayana.

they die. So how did we come up with a risk-based retirement savings system? Whose bright idea was it? Does financial peril "from cradle to grave" make any logical sense? Is peril and risk the advice you would instinctively recommend to a loved one approaching their *fixed-income* retirement years?

Today, a common mantra of Wall Street investment advisers is "You're in this for the long haul." When you think about it, this statement becomes rather laughable during retirement. Long haul? Really? What long haul are they speaking of? For the average person, retirement comes at a point in life where one's "long haul" becomes exponentially shorter with each passing year. For a majority of retirees, the first ten years of retirement will be the best ten years they have left.

Certainly, retirement deserves a better-suited strategic mantra than "You're in it for the long haul." In fact, perhaps a far more appropriate retirement mantra should sound like, "It's now or never, baby!" Who wants to reduce income withdrawals and forfeit lifestyle pleasures during the best 10 years of health and vitality they have remaining? Most retirees will have the greatest capacity to live life to the fullest with health, vitality, vim and vigor during their first decade of retirement. At age 60, one does not anticipate being able to run faster at age 70. At age 80, one may not anticipate making a run at all! Wouldn't it be better to secure peace of mind and ensure our ability to enjoy our money while we can still "think, feel, spit, and chew," rather than when we might only be able to "sleep and slobber"? Even better, how about a plan that allows for both! Why not have a plan that allows us to spend our money now without the fear of running out tomorrow? Why not retire with a plan for *IN-come* versus a plan for *IF-come?*

Financial planning advice that may lead to either a suspension or a reduction of income for the better part of a decade in order to ride out a market collapse may make sense to an adviser earning a fee on our assumption of risk, but it does not make sense for the one paying the price for that assumption. It is easy for Wall Street to tell us "we're in it for the long haul." But the truth is that our retirement years are precious years; and for most of us, they are years with little margin for financial error. If ever there were years to avoid financial risk, surely these are those years! For those who lack true multigenerational wealth, retirement savings should never be left to financial risk and peril!

Why would anyone truly interested in *our* best chance for success try to convince us otherwise?

Life as a Financial Road Trip

Tom Cochrane once said, "Life is a highway." So let's look at our financial life as a road trip! In the early years, the road may have been a dirt road full of gravel, dust, and mud holes. It was hard to make good time (savings) while on that road. Finally, you made it off of those early entry-level roads. You turned onto a well-paved road called an interstate highway. Boy, did you make good time (savings) while cruising down the financial interstate! Eventually, though, financial reflexes became slower. Financial wounds took longer to heal. One day, you decided life on this dangerous high-speed financial interstate was no longer comfortable. It was time to take a slower-paced, safe, peaceful, scenic path. You exit the highway and embark on the final stretch of financial road you will travel during your lifetime.

Up ahead, you notice a fork in the road. As you approach, you realize that each fork leads to a long, narrow bridge crossing a perilously deep ravine.

This was not the sort of excitement you were hoping to encounter at this stage of your financial road journey! The bridges are narrow, without guardrails. You consider turning back. But Father Time will not permit you that option. So, with no small measure of caution, you approach the fork. You notice a sign stating:

"Welcome, Financial Traveler. Only one leg of this journey is left. Choose well which bridge you cross, as not all bridges are built by reputable builders, nor constructed with sturdy materials guaranteed to support you as you cross."

What? Really? Are you kidding me? Okay. You stop the car and walk toward the first bridge. You are determined to inspect each bridge. What are its materials? Does the architectural firm that designed it have a stellar track record? Is its construction crew trustworthy? Everything within you screams, "This is not the time to flip a coin, call 'heads,' and hope for the best!"

This book is written so you won't have to flip that coin as you enter the final phase of your financial life: the distribution phase of retirement. It reveals the history of the people and processes who constructed the "financial bridges" we must choose from as we commit to the final leg of life's financial journey. Retirement really is like a narrow, one-way bridge. For most of us, once we are on that bridge, making a successful U-turn is simply not a survivable option! There is no do-over in retirement. You need to be sure that the financial bridge you've chosen for retirement will not collapse on you, nor your spouse, before you *both* make it to the other side!

How We Arrived "Here"

For most of us, our financial "here" probably has a lot to do with an IRA, 401k, or equivalent tax-qualified savings plan. Today, almost all employer-sponsored defined contribution plans are tax-qualified: 401k, 403b, SEP, SIMPLE, Self-directed IRA, a Keogh, and so on. These accounts are "tax qualified" in that unique tax laws govern how these accounts work during the contribution and distribution periods. We will discuss the potential impact of these unique rules in a later chapter. For now, let's just say a reasonable person, when evaluating the pros and cons of such tax laws, might agree with Ed Slott—a CPA and multiple *New York Times* bestselling author—when he likens them to a *Retirement Ticking Time Bomb!*[14]

According to a highly regarded research study published in 2013 by the Investment Company Institute, more than 67% of all working households own some sort of tax qualified saving account. Interestingly, that number increases

---

14 Ed Slott, *The Retirement Savings Time Bomb… And How to Diffuse It*, Penguin Books (2007).

with age, since baby boomers own the vast majority of funds held in these accounts today.[15] Nearly all the people I talk with on my weekly radio show or at my private financial retirement seminars have at least one such tax-qualified account. Exceptions are truly rare.

Astoundingly, the vast majority of people I meet with have **over 90% of their entire life's liquid cash savings** wrapped up in these accounts. For instance, if a client with a $1,000,000 liquid net worth pulled out a cash liquidity statement, here's how the numbers would break down:

- $900,000 in a tax qualified account
- $100,000 sitting in a bank checking account, savings account, wallet, or mattress

Tax qualified accounts have become pervasive in our culture. If a person has saved for retirement, they have likely done so primarily by funding a tax-qualified account.

[Note: I say "*if* a person has saved" because the same ICI report published in 2013 revealed that 33% of all households contribute to neither an IRA nor any employer-sponsored retirement plan.[16] I wonder: Could that be because the middle class has effectively not had its average income (wage) increased for the last eighteen years? And perhaps this same lack of wage growth is part of why nearly a third of millennials between the ages of 18 and 34 are still living with their parents? With stagnant incomes and rising costs, members of this generation have few options of how to save for a down payment on a house of their own.]

For many baby boomers, a tax-qualified account is not merely their *primary* retirement savings vehicle—it is their *only* one! Few in the public sector today have guaranteed pensions of any significance. Treasure them if you do!

---

15 Investment Company Institute, "The Role of IRAs in U.S. Households' Saving for Retirement, 2013," November 2013. Accessed May 15, 2018 at https://www.ici.org/pdf/per19-11.pdf.

16 Ibid.

Funding Retirement – What Choice Do We Have?

Your tax-qualified account is risky. When you opened it, the options available for funding it were likely Wall Street securities instruments: stocks, bonds, mutual funds. Of course, all those options are risky. Most employer-sponsored plans have no guaranteed safe money investment options. Don't believe me? Go to your employer-sponsored 401k plan and try to locate an alternative non-securities safe money investment option. Just don't hold your breath while you're looking! Unless you are a state or federal government employee, chances are it doesn't exist.

I know all of this risk-based equities investment strategy might sound normal today. After all, where else would people invest for their futures? Surely not a bank passbook savings account, or a CD savings account—both paying zero point something for interest. Good luck with that! So, risk it is! As everyone knows, "without risk there is no reward."

It didn't used to be this way. Things are much different today than most of us would have imagined just a single generation ago. The truth is, for most of our nation's history, fewer than one in ten Americans ever invested a single penny in a risk-based Wall Street stock, corporate bond, or mutual fund. In 1980, just over 12% of all Americans owned such risky financial products.[17] Stunning by today's standards, isn't it?

Consider the Great Depression era. In 1929, *only about 1% of working Americans had any money invested in the stock market*.[18] Consequently, very few Americans actually lost money directly in the market crash of 1929–1933. Only the wealthy had invested in the stock market. At the time, the stock market was called the "Wall Street Casino." Why? Because that's where the super wealthy went to *speculate* with money they didn't need. *Play* money, if you will. What we might call "casino money"!

Wealthy people speculated in the stock market, but they generally didn't place huge chunks of their family's wealth at risk. Why embrace risk in hope

---

17 Harry Dent, *The Next Great Bubble Boom*, 292. Free Press.

18 "The 1920s Statistics," Accessed May 15, 2018 at https://www.shmoop.com/1920s/statistics.html.

of additional wealth when you already have wealth? Wealthy people rarely become wealthy by following such foolishness.

So how *did* the market's crash ignite the Great Depression? Essentially, the stock market crash triggered a domino effect. Those dominos began to hit the U.S. banking industry in a huge wave. Back then, banks were allowed to invest (speculate) their customers' cash deposits into market-based financial assets (Wall Street stocks). And invest they did—quite heavily!

When ordinary people learned that the market was in a free-fall crash, and recalled that the banks had invested *their deposits* into the stock market, they panicked. A historic "run" on bank deposits began. The federal government eventually stepped in and declared "bank holidays"—a period in which one cannot withdraw money. But it was too late. Banks had already lost a fortune as the stock market lost 90% of its value. Nearly ten thousand banks filed for bankruptcy. Their downfall also meant the downfall of tens of thousands of companies, along with millions of middle-class people. Bank deposits were not FDIC insured at that time.

Imagine waking up tomorrow to this reality: Banks are out of money—your money! We get the term "bankruptcy" from the root words "bank" and "rupture." That's exactly what happened in the Great Depression: banks ruptured! In the end, it didn't matter if you had your money in the market, or in the bank. It vanished either way.

So people were flat broke. And not just a few people—millions. Prices fell because no one had any money. That's what causes a depression: lack of money, or else an abundance of money concentrated in the hands of a very few. Either will do the trick. Historically, the two usually accompany each other, and both were true during the Great Depression. Truly rich people seem to never lose their money. Those with multigenerational wealth seem to always get richer with every financial collapse in history. Such was the case during The Great Depression. Fortunes were made during that time because not *everybody* was broke. The rich stayed rich. But the average, everyday people in the middle class and below became accustomed to bread and soup lines.

People today worry about inflation. Inflation can be painful. However, there is a major difference between an *inflationary* period and a *deflationary* period.

An inflationary period is characterized by an abundance of money. Too much money, too fast! Nevertheless, during inflationary periods, people do *have* money. How else could they go to the grocery store and buy a loaf of bread with the proverbial wheelbarrow full of money? We saw literal pictures of hyperinflation occurring in Germany during the time preceding the rise of Adolf Hitler and his Nazi Party. Wheelbarrows of money existed in Germany because the masses actually did have a lot of (nearly worthless) money—hyperinflation.

On the other hand, a deflationary period is characterized by a lack of money. The year 1929 become the catalyst of the Great Depression because people, and companies, were broke. Remember what we said earlier: Most people did not lose their money in the stock market. Only 1% of Americans invested directly in the stock market.

Stop and think about what that means. If 99% of people did not invest in the stock market, *where were they saving for their future?* Well, for over 200 years of our nation's history, people saved for their future with traditional "safe money" strategies. Today, these same strategies are loathed by Wall Street and its army of financial salespeople, conveniently labeled as "Financial "Advisers." Loathsome as these archaic safe money strategies may be by Wall Street standards, people used to do quite well while investing in them. Before banks were allowed to risk deposits into stock equities, people received a reasonable interest rate with security for their deposits.

Then Wall Street turned everything upside down. Even the smart people at the bank couldn't manage, control, or predict the ups and downs (risk) inherent within the stock market! Shortly after the crash and collapse of the banking industry, the FDIC bank insurance system was created to ensure safety for the bank savings of the common working man—or at least so we are told.

Realize that the FDIC didn't actually fix the banking system. Fixing it would have meant forcing banks to *be responsible* with our cash deposits and limiting them to *low-risk investments*. After the effects of The Great Depression, you'd think this would have been the law forever! But that did not happen. The financial elite are extraordinarily powerful in Washington, D.C., and they like to gamble with OPM (Other People's Money). Our money! So Congress did not tell banks, "No more risky gambling forever." Instead, Congress—bought and paid for by Wall Street bankers—passed legislation to insure the banks for future losses! They can still gamble with your money, but you won't take the fall if they fail. Tax payers will. Oh wait. You and I are the tax payers. How convenient. Wall Street got Congress to write laws that force us (taxpayers) to guarantee their ability to risk and lose our money—at our expense!

Back to banks. We've learned that banks were one of the primary places people would save and store money. Was there anyplace else "normal" people saved for their future? Think hard…. I'll bet you're having a hard time coming up with one, aren't you? Okay, I'll let you off the hook. Try *life insurance companies*!

Most people today don't consider life insurance companies to be a prime place to use to save for their future retirement. On the contrary, they've been taught to think of life insurance products as perhaps a necessary evil, but certainly not a sound savings or investment strategy. But again, **it didn't used to be this way!**

Before tax-qualified laws came into existence, life insurance companies were commonly where the average American saved for his financial future. And the life insurance company also protected the family's *present* financial need, should something terrible cut short the life of its primary breadwinner(s).

People today are familiar with JC Penny, the department store. However, a lot of younger people today might not know that JC Penny was a real person. He was a real person who went through the real Great Depression. However, unlike many others, he did not go broke during it. Rather, JC Penny came out with a fortune! How? JC (like other business tycoons) survived because there was one place he'd been stuffing his extra cash—quite a lot of it. When the Great Depression hit, his money was in this place, **still growing and still there for him.** What place might it have been? A *whole life insurance policy* that accumulated cash value. Of all the places JC Penny kept money, *cash value life insurance* proved to be the most reliable. That cash in his policies allowed JC to build his business. He could buy up virtually anything he wanted for pennies on the dollar, turning his business into a juggernaut. Imagine having access to cash when virtually no one else does! JC Penny had cash when most people didn't, and that made him rich.

You see, true wealth is not determined by how many dollars one has. True wealth is determined by the amount of dollars one has, contrasted with the amount of dollars others have. You could be wealthy with a single dollar in your pocket—if no one else had a dollar in their pocket!

Wealthy people get wealthier because they never lose their cash savings. Poor people get poorer because they keep losing their cash savings. Cash makes all the difference. Perhaps a salient lesson for those of us about to enter our retirement years?

Back to the stock market….

The stock market offers the *potential* of financial gain. But it also has a history of the opposite: taking people's cash and making it disappear! It has happened repeatedly throughout history. Everybody knows it. No one denies it. It was for this reason that a vast majority of Americans used to stay completely out of the stock market. It lacked the certainty people want and need when saving for their future.

Nevertheless, safe money savings strategies began to fade. Mystifyingly, these trusted **200-year old strategies**—backed by the world's most historically stable financial institutions, many of which are more than a century old—these stalwart, tried-and-true strategies began to be abandoned. Even more mysteriously, this change seemed to coincide precisely with the advent of our ubiquitous friend, the tax qualified savings plan—the 401k and IRA of today.

Where did tax qualified plans originate? Was it a grassroots idea whose time had simply come? Were people upset with the prospect of safely retiring on the three-legged stool of Social Security, guaranteed company pensions, and personal saving strategies, all built upon the foundation of safe and guaranteed growth? Were ordinary people demanding change?

Or was there something else at play?

The Marriage of Wall Street and Uncle Sam

Tax-deferred savings plans were the joint brainchild of Wall Street and Congress, not of the grassroots working man. In their early years, these plans were not popularly used or even widely accepted by the working man. In fact, when first presented, they were originally available only to wealthy C-Level executives as a way for them to shelter some of their present income from taxation in the here and now. Wall Street kept beating the drum advocating for them, as did Wall Street's propaganda machine: the mainstream media. In the end, the relentless pounding of Wall Street propaganda touting the promised benefits of the IRA and 401k for the "average man" won out.

What was the effect of the partnership between Wall Street and Congress? How clearly did their combined scheme to invent a securities-risk–based, tax-qualified, retirement savings vehicle work? People are amazed when I show them the truth, as I am about to show you with the following chart. This chart was taken originally from Yahoo Finance, then enhanced with comments for dramatic purposes in an attempt to tell its story. The chart represents the history of the S&P 500 Stock Index. This index is widely considered the most accurate measure of the broader U.S. economy. It represents the 500 most widely-traded large cap companies across a wide spectrum of U.S. industry sectors.

Remarkably, many people tell me they have never been shown anything like this historic chart before meeting with me. That makes sense if one has only ever received financial advice from a Wall Street financial adviser who makes a living selling securities-based products (products of risk like stocks, bonds, and mutual funds).

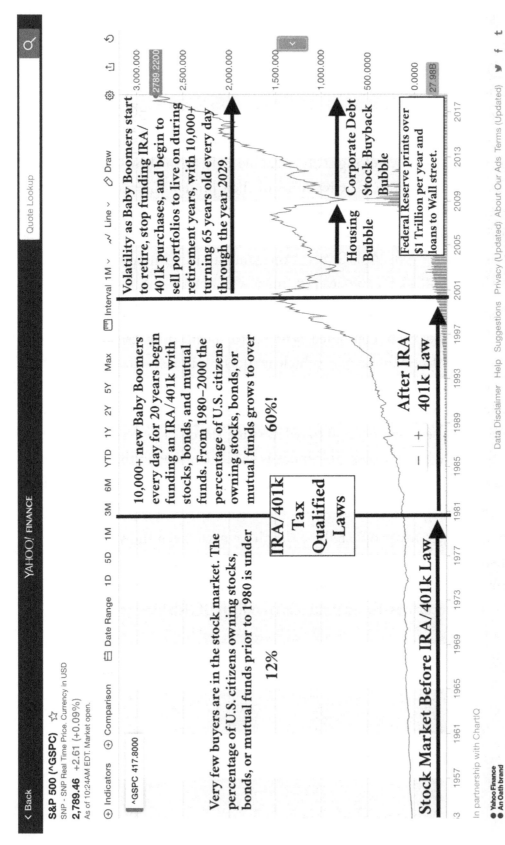

Stock Market Before IRA/401k Law

Very few buyers are in the stock market. The percentage of U.S. citizens owning stocks, bonds, or mutual funds prior to 1980 is under

12%

IRA/401k
Tax
Qualified
Laws

10,000+ new Baby Boomers every day for 20 years begin funding an IRA/401k with stocks, bonds, and mutual funds. From 1980–2000 the percentage of U.S. citizens owning stocks, bonds, or mutual funds grows to over

60%!

After IRA/401k Law

Volatility as Baby Boomers start to retire, stop funding IRA/401k purchases, and begin to sell portfolios to live on during retirement years, with 10,000+ turning 65 years old every day through the year 2029.

Housing Bubble

Corporate Debt Stock Buyback Bubble

Federal Reserve prints over $1 Trillion per year and loans to Wall street.

[Note: Have you ever thought about this? The Wall Street financial world named these products of risk "securities." Let me say that again. Products of "risk" are actually called "securities" by Wall Street! Does anyone else see the irony? You can't make this stuff up! Even the nomenclature created by Wall Street's financial elite leads one to embrace a false sense of "security." Does it not? The Book of Isaiah says, "Woe unto them that call evil good, and good evil." I wonder what it would say about those who decided to call products of risk "securities"? To be clear, there is nothing wrong with risk—so long as the one risking understands it to be risky! The deceptive name is the issue.]

So, why would a purveyor of risk not want you to see the above chart? Perhaps because, even with a cursory glance, it raises several obvious and uncomfortable questions:

1. Why was the market a flat boring market for decades?

2. What happed around 1980 that caused this relatively flat market to come alive and begin to grow in such a historically unprecedented way?

3. What happened around the year 2000 that transformed the market from 20 years of "Steady Eddie" to a new era of "Scary Kerry"?

4. Mr. Securities Broker Sales Person, can you explain to me why I should continue to ride the "Scary Kerry" rollercoaster of risk throughout my retirement while my entire life savings hangs in the balance?

Pictures paint a thousand words, don't they? It's especially true with this chart! If we take the time to look, then muster the courage to believe what our eyes see, the truth illustrated in this chart stares us square in the eye. The market can go up, and the market can go down. It can stay up for a while. It can stay down for a while. However, "a while" is a relative time period—particularly when one compares working-age years with retirement years!

The Underlying Value of a Stock

What truly drives the underlying value of any individual stock in the market? The answer is not rocket science. But it is also not what most of us have been led to believe. When one boils it all down, the answer is a matter of simple math. Specifically, the kind of math I call "people" math. Others have labeled it "demographical math." This is the math we're going to look at extensively in the next two chapters.

What if there were a historically accurate way of mathematically predicting the *economic headwinds* that influence the underlying value of a developed country's economy and markets? Perhaps the very kind of math that Wall Street's financial elite seem to know and benefit from? We'll soon see…. That math may actually exist!

How's our little financial *conspiratorial theory* going? Can you say "tip of the iceberg"?

Chapter Four.

Every Explosion Needs a Catalyst: Enter the 401k

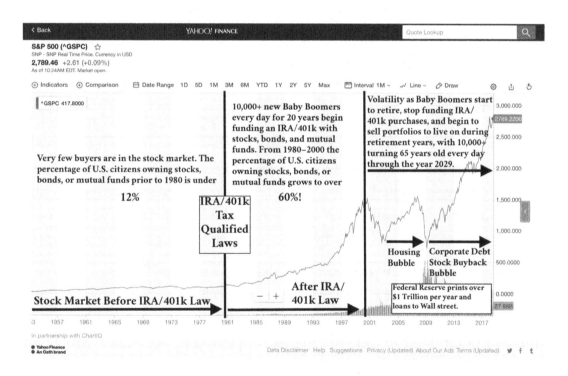

Remarkable, isn't it? You literally can draw a line down the middle of time where two historic realities converged to mark the explosion of the previously dormant and boring stock market. It's a distinct change so obvious no one can deny it. One side of the explosion is the Pre-401k/IRA era, and the other is the Post-401k/IRA era. The transition marks the awakening of our modern stock market experience. Make no mistake: this was not a random act of kindness fortuitously timed by the "chance awakening" of a suddenly benevolent-minded stock market. Far from it. The explosion in this market was engineered, and the timing couldn't have been more *fortuitously planned*—for the wealthy on Wall Street.

Everyone knows that explosions don't just happen in a nothingness vacuum (unless, of course, one really is God)! Every explosion needs a catalyst. This is a hard law of physics. There are no exceptions. **Once we identify the catalyst that produced the explosion of growth that has occurred in the stock market over the last 30 years, we will be better qualified to intelligently predict where that same market may take us for the next 30 years—the bridge spanning retirement for baby boomers!**

History indicates there were two elements that, when combined, created the catalyst for the stock market's sudden explosion. The first element we will consider now. The second we will look at in Chapter Six.

So what was the first element? You have probably guessed it by now. The **re-writing of income tax laws** which created the new tax-qualified savings vehicles. This ushered in the *Era of the 401k and IRA*.

If you are a member of the ruling class, how do you control and manipulate the underclass? How do you get them to do what you want them to do with their money? (By the way, this always means giving their money back to its rightful owner—the elite!) How do you make the underclass buy into an idea which ultimately serves to empower the ruling class in perpetuity? Moreover, how do you get them to do this by exercising a choice of their own free will?

Simple. You convince the underclass that *they are the real winners*. You focus their attention on "what's in it for them." Once individuals believe an idea is in their self-interest, from that moment on they will act upon it for *their* reasons. The end result is no forced will and, consequently, no resistance. Just blind, willing, enthusiastic obedience without end!

In our story of financial system histories, the tax-deferred savings plan (401k, IRA, etc.) became just the trick!

Time to Bait the Tax Hook

Nobody likes paying taxes. The elite hate paying taxes so much they create loop holes in the tax system laws. These allow them, and the companies they own, to generate billions of dollars in wealth and often still not pay a single penny in taxes.

Despite righteously complaining about the rich not paying taxes, we normal folk truly envy them. We have always wanted to be like the rich in this regard. Of course, the rich know this. So, why not give the "ordinary" people what they want: a tax break! Allow them to think they are finally "getting one over" on old Uncle Sam—just like the rich.

"But, of course," say the financial elite, "we don't want them to actually be like us and not pay taxes. So how do we give them the appearance of a tax advantage, without the actual substance?" Translation: How do we do this without *really* giving them a true "tax win"? The answer: through a cleverly-designed system called a tax-qualified savings plan.

Said the Wall Street elite: "We'll frame the rules of this newfangled retirement savings tool as a way to 'get one over' on Uncle Sam! Of course, contributions to these accounts must be limited, because good things (for the little guy) always have limits. Plus, placing a limitation on a specific thing increases desire for that very thing! People always want what they can't have. Once this table is set, and self-centered greed kicks in, watch people flock like geese to hand over the use and control of their entire life savings to its rightful owners—us. The elite. The rightful owners of wealth!"

[Note: Think about it. Who actually has use and control of our money when it's invested in a stock, bond, or mutual fund? Answer: Only two entities. The company we invested in and, to a lesser degree, the brokerage house via the fee paid to it while it is invested. We may think we have control. But in reality, our control over that money is the same as our control over the money we might place on a bet at a craps table in the casino. Once bet, the dice and the house are now in control, not us! Try taking that money off the table and putting it back into your pocket while the dice are still in play! You'll quickly find out who has control of that money. I promise, it isn't you or me! We don't get the opportunity to take back control of that money until we've been declared a winner. But to benefit from the winning, we have to **stop playing and cash out our winnings**. Similarly, in order to win with stocks, one must "cash out" by selling and removing the money from the market. Walmart will not accept a brokerage statement as a form of payment! It takes real money to buy something at Walmart. From the moment we purchase a stock, we literally **give up control and use of our money**—until the moment we sell that stock and cash out by taking our money out of the market. Make no mistake, however. *Someone* is benefiting while we've given up control—it's just not us! We may win. We may not win. There is nothing illegal here. Just buyer beware.... The market is a gamble. And, *in the interim, we have no use or control of our money!*]

For the elite bankers on Wall Street, the plan was beginning to flesh itself out. "Convince the masses they're finally getting one over on the tax man. Plus, why not allow them to get a small matching donation from their employer? If we give them a little *free* money and structure it so they don't *feel* like they're paying taxes on it, they will never think about saving through any other strategy. Who has the will to walk away from 'free' money?"

[Note: Casinos (owned by the Elite) also use this strategy to entice people to gamble in their house of chance when they offer free matching "house money" coupons.]

"In fact, they'll so love the free money and the *feeling* of not paying taxes on it that we can probably get away with charging them an ongoing fee for the privilege of handing their money to us. Maybe we can establish a fee structure large enough to pay for the millions of lower-level sales advocates we'll need to execute this masterful plan on our behalf! After all, why should we pay for these sales people out of our pockets? Let's make the underclass pay for them! We'll call these low-level advocates 'financial advisers' instead of 'sales representatives' because calling them 'financial advisers' makes them sound so much more trustworthy and intelligent. Even though they have no idea what tomorrow brings, a certification from the "official" regulatory bodies we create will convince the average investor that they do!"

Feeling a bit duped yet?

It was a masterful plan!

[Note: For the record, I don't know if any of the above conversations historically ever took place. Let's hope not. Let's hope the people who actually own the gold, and, make our laws and rules as a result, do not think and plan in such diabolical ways. But it is kind of interesting that the whole fictional conversation closely lines up with the end result of what has *actually happened* in real life. Coincidence? Another one of those "Hmmm…" moments.]

The planning and implementation of this "controlled" market explosion beginning with the tax qualified 401k/IRA era took several decades. It did not happen overnight. But in the end, the money, power, and influence of the financial elite won over the votes of congressional representatives. Simultaneously, the media elite (owned by the financial elite of Wall Street) began to saturate the middle-class with risk-based retirement savings propaganda. This IRA propaganda, of course, paraded only the positive *opportunities* for wealth accumulation heralded by these new retirement investment strategies. What is worse, the media elite emphasized that these opportunities for wealth accumulation would be best managed by a "certified" and licensed Wall Street financial planning firm. Both Wall Street and Congress, through the media, immediately began to sell this paradigm shift in retirement savings planning to the public. Almost overnight, the relative "have-nots" began handing their hard-earned life savings and financial future over to the "have-a-lots," the Wall Street elite. We even paid a fee to Wall Street for the privilege of placing our life savings in a perpetual position of risk! We, the have-nots, proved to be the proverbial cheap date. A *temporary* tax deferral and a *small* matching donation is all it took. Greed can be both blinding and powerful. When greed struck: Voila! The IRA and 401k laws of today were born, and here comes the *modern* stock market era boom. No one bothered to inform us of the long-term price we would ultimately pay.

What We Unwittingly Gave Up

Little did we realize the tradeoff that would follow. In reality, our two-century-old safe money savings systems were now under assault. That assault would eventually lead to:

1. The practical death of the private pension.

2. The practical death of the passbook savings account as a meaningful method of saving and growing wealth.

3. The practical death of the CD as a meaningful savings tool.

4. The death of permanent cash value life insurance policies as a desirable means by which those in the *underclass* saved for their future.

Every safe money investment was about to be slowly but methodically destroyed over the next 35 years.

Think about it. In 1980, what were the interest rates offered to savers of that time? Almost 16%! Contrast this with today's interest rates nearly a generation later: zero point something. Hmmm. Another coincidence?

Consider the chart below, which tracks the history of the US Ten Year Treasury Note interest rate. Since the high of almost 16% in the early 1980s, the trajectory has been nothing short of a planned race to zero! One cannot look at what has happened to guaranteed safe-money savings strategies and come to any other rational conclusion.

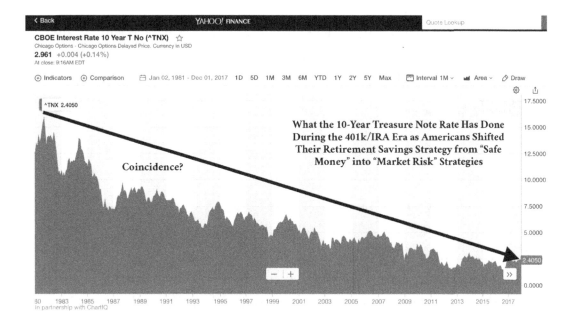

Coincidentally, these near-zero interest rates arrived just in time to prevent baby boomers from rolling their substantial retirement savings into a safe haven alternative. Today, baby boomers have no place to store their accumulated wealth and receive a reasonable rate of return without having to carry the 100% risk of loss imposed by the stock market. These low interest rates struck in the very hour baby boomers needed to avoid risk and losses the most: retirement! This is the system Wall Street and Uncle Sam created—for Wall Street and Uncle Sam. Truly, one has to wonder: Who is really winning here? Is it you and me? Or Wall Street and Uncle Sam? Fewer and fewer people still trust this system—along with the benevolent-minded people who created and advocate for it. Millions of baby boomers are beginning to wake up and say, "no more"!

Think it through. Safe, guaranteed, *meaningful* interest rates for middle class savers ... completely gone. When? At just the time those who had spent the last 30 years risking and saving for retirement would need their money to be safe and preserved the most.

If you are inclined to enjoy a good conspiracy theory, the story gets even better. Even if you are not such a person, you still must admit that this gigantic "coincidence" heavily favors the wealthy elite of Wall Street. The flow of money to them from the middle class is now likely to stay around in perpetuity. What choice do we have? Place our savings in a zero point something interest-bearing account?

Could it really be a conspiracy? Surely not. Those well-meaning, globalist Wall Street elite along with their bought-and-paid-for lawmakers ... they would never do anything like this to the rest of us working folk. Never!

And yet, here we stand.

The Upside Down Financial System

In the 1980s, interest rates began their never-before-seen-in-the-history-of-the-world, three-decade-long descent to zero. Meanwhile, the financial elite switched from **paying** everyday savers for the use of their hard-earned savings **to being paid fees** by those savers for storing and investing their money! Think about it. Wall Street bankers succeeded in flipping the entire financial system upside down. When is the last time you didn't have to pay a fee to put away savings in your 401k, or IRA, or any form of money in the stock market—even when you lose? Why does Wall Street not win if we win and lose when we lose? Or, at the very least, not make money when we lose? We've been trained and conditioned to believe that the job of a Wall Street financial adviser is to manage our money so that we make money. Yet the very way in which this person is compensated strongly suggests this is not true. Even when we lose money the adviser is paid. Where else can you hold a job that pays you if you fail to do what your boss believes he hired you to do? Only on Wall Street! You see, the dirty little truth is actually quite simple. The structure of compensation tells us this simple truth. A Wall Street advisor is not paid to make his client money. A Wall Street advisor is paid (incentivized) to keep his client's money in a position of perpetual risk, *where the adviser and his firm can make money!*

Fees are the lifeblood of the Wall Street system. This is why they never want us to sell and take our "winnings" and make them permanent by removing them from the market.

Today, we are so accustomed to paying fees on our money that we don't even blink at fees on our bank checking or savings accounts. Talk about adding insult to injury and rubbing salt in a wound! The bank charges us fees, and in return gives us interest of zero point something while making over 20% interest in credit card account loans. Am I the only person who sees this as immoral?

The elite on Wall Street have established a financial system that ensures their power and wealth at the expense of working-class people, relegating the working class to a perpetual place of public debt and serfdom. Why is there so little uproar? Is it because we've hopped on the stock market bus with them, and now we don't want (or can't afford) to see it crash? It's hard to criticize others' decisions once you've adopted them as your own. Even though our 401k system keeps the financial elite wealthy and gives them enormous power over us, we don't want to see our 401k crash or disappear. It's a vicious circle. (This is one reason why the Wall Street elite hardly ever go to jail, and why no one complains too much when we bail out the scoundrels with public debt money.)

Since we've volunteered to take a seat on the Wall Street stock market bus. Let's try to understand what drives this bus and the stock prices we encounter while on it.

Part II.

Understanding Market Dynamics: What Drives Stock Price Values

Chapter Five.

What Really Drives Stock Prices? Truth and Fiction

Give the Devil His Due

During the first 20 years of the 401k and IRA savings strategy, Wall Street and its army of financial advisers were right. Financial advisers seemed like financial gods. From 1980 to 2000, the S&P 500 stock market indices with dividends reinvested averaged 17.4% growth per year.[19]

Think about that for a minute.

What impact would 17.4% percent *average* growth per year **for 20 years** have on the public investor's psyche? Might 20 years of 17.4% average returns convince investors (you and I) that the stock market was the absolute greatest place between here and Mars to throw and grow money? Might it eliminate the notion that buying risk-based "securities" is actually an act of speculative

---

19   DQYDJ, "S&P 500 Return Calculator, with Dividend Reinvestment," May 6, 2018. Accessed May 15, 2018 at https://dqydj.com/sp-500-return-calculator/.

gambling, rather than sound money investing? Might it establish a mindset that investing in risky instruments (stocks, bonds, and mutual funds) is paradoxically somehow predictable and manageable, and therefore "preferable" to guaranteed safe money investing strategies? And finally, might it lead the common investor to respect and trust the unparalleled sagacity of their Wall Street financial adviser? By the year 2000, might these advisers and the institutions behind them be regarded as near god-like financial geniuses?

Many readers will remember the famous slogan of a popular financial TV commercial that aired back in the early- to mid-1980s:

"When E.F. Hutton talks ... people listen."

The clever commercial showed a room full of people at a dinner party, all engaged in various conversations. At least until one man cleared his throat and began to speak. Then, the entire room of well-dressed, highly-educated professionals instantly became silent in mid-sentence. Who was this man? The adviser from E.F. Hutton, of course. A financial god was about to bless them with superior insight and knowledge! No one could afford to miss it.

In truth, neither E.F. Hutton nor the advisers who worked for him were financial gods. Not one of them owned a working crystal ball. However, the commercial does reveal how the Wall Street elite want us to think. They want us to believe that there *are* financial gods, that *they* are those gods, and that we have nothing to worry about as long as we trust them. "The peril of financial risk has no power over the financial gods!"

Excuse me while I run to the bathroom.

In 2008, the CBS Sunday evening magazine show "60 Minutes" did an exposé on the merits of the 401k retirement system. At the time of writing, one can still view the interview clip by visiting https://youtu.be/zw3JoJXkHZk.

Every retired person, and every person approaching retirement in the next five years, should be required to watch that clip. In fact, you should watch it right now before reading the next paragraph! It is a tear-jerking reminder of how devastating and permanent financial risk can be when loss comes at the wrong time: near, at, or in retirement!

Why was the stock market crash of 2008 so alarming? Because it was the second time in less than 10 years that the market had destroyed the retirement accounts of millions of people who had spent the last 30 years of their lives diligently saving. Now, finally needing to live off those savings, these savers discovered their money was gone. But not really gone. You see, in a financial transaction, money never disappears. It just moves from one individual's pocket to another's. Your and my money disappeared because someone else **sold trillions of dollars' worth of stock**, causing demand—and thus value—to be reduced greatly. However, contrary to the talking heads on the mainstream media, your wealth didn't disappear in 2008. It was taken—by those who sold!

The end result of the 2000 and 2008 historic market crashes was the same. Millions of just-retired people lost any hope of maintaining their planned lifestyle and/or enjoying retirement without having to return to work of some form. Many returned to work at places like McDonalds and Walmart, earning far less than before they retired. Their old job was either gone or taken by a younger and less expensive worker. A double bonus for Wall Street. Not only did the Elite initiate a massive sell off resulting in a huge taking of profit by those at the top, they benefited on the back end by a net lowering of wages, the major cost associated with holding down corporate profits in the future! Everybody won at the top. Did you win? Did your neighbor win? Conversely, how many people lost jobs and/or were forced to work several more years, giving up what should have been the best years of their retirement?

In the aftermath of both crashes this century, millions could no longer afford to retire at all. They continued to work well into their seventies, some even into their eighties. In some cases, these are the people we still see greeting us as we walk into Walmart! I promise you, working at Walmart into one's 80s was not a part of anyone's original retirement plan! Yet, after all the financial pain inflicted by Wall Street's "ideal retirement plan system," rather than reform retirement **income** strategies, the Wall Street financial planning industrial complex continued to bombard people with the same old tired advice: "Be patient.... Wait it out.... You're in this for the long haul! This too shall pass. It's only a paper loss...." In time, Wall Street regained the public's confidence. Average individuals decided to continue funding their 401ks and IRAs, maintaining a position of financial risk from cradle to grave. After all, "Risk is nothing to be feared. Risk can be efficiently managed. The peril of risk can be avoided or controlled if you just have the right financial adviser!"

Where's that bathroom again?

Call me crazy, but … **that's not what the dictionary says about risk.** Here are some of the definitions you will find when you look for "risk" in a dictionary:

- Possibility of loss or injury;
- a situation involving exposure to danger;
- someone or something that creates or suggests a hazard;
- the chance that an investment (such as a stock or commodity) will lose value.

Do you see anything on this list that brings comfort or peace of mind? Not a single image conveyed is one I would run to embrace. Particularly during years of retirement!

Look up synonyms for "risk" and you'll find them equally concerning:

- Chance
- Uncertainty
- Unpredictability
- Precariousness
- Instability
- Insecurity
- Perilousness

What do those definitions and synonyms tell us about risk? They scream at us! Listen:

"**All risk is serious!** Risk, by definition, **IS 100% RISK!** Safety, peace of mind, predictability—none of these are anywhere to be found in RISK!"

This, of course, is the exact opposite of what a Wall Street broker wants us to think as we leave our life savings under his "*control*."

Shouldn't we be trying to condition people to *avoid* rather than *embrace* risk? Especially people who are in or approaching retirement—a time when risk and loss are no longer tolerable!

A prudent investor who is about to retire might aptly think of risk in the following manner: According to the definition of risk, risk is loss, injury, danger, and hazard all knocking at one's front door together. It's like having a gang of murdering financial robbers, thugs, and thieves standing outside your home. Honestly, in that situation, would you "risk" opening the door? Not me! I'm locking the door and barring it shut! Seems like the only logical strategy.

Yet the Wall Street financial planning industrial complex would have us believe that we should leave our financial doors unlocked, or worse, standing wide open! They train us to accept the false idea that risk is good. Somehow, living in a permanent, perpetual position of financial risk is not a problem—as long as we pay them to manage it! After all, the financial gods can handle risk.

It amazes me how pervasively Wall Street has been able to ingrain this insidious belief into the mindset of so many approaching retirement today.

Case in Point

As I was writing this chapter, a gentleman called me. Let's name him "Mike," and his wife "Carla." Mike and Carla had attended one of my private retirement planning seminars. Afterward, they scheduled an appointment to meet with me. It was December 2017, the market was riding an all-time high, and Mike was about to retire at the end of the year.

When I met with Mike and Carla, they told me that in order to maintain their desired lifestyle in retirement, they needed an income of $7,284 per month. Their current sources of guaranteed income, like Social Security and pensions, totaled $5,661 per month. Thus, the gap between their current and desired financial state was $1,623 per month of after-tax income—$19,476 per year. This is what Mike and Carla needed in order to bridge the gap and guarantee that their *basic* living expense needs would be met in retirement.

Over the years, I have found that for the vast majority of those I meet with who have been able to save for retirement, at least 90% of their entire liquid cash life savings are tied up in a tax-qualified account. This means 90% of their liquid cash assets are 100% at risk in the "securities" market. Mike and Carla were part of that vast majority. Their total liquid cash net worth was $870,000. Of that, $838,000 was in various tax-qualified savings plans—all of which were 100% at risk in the market. After a lifetime of savings, Mike and Carla only kept $32,000 in cash savings or cash-equivalent accounts outside the market. This meant that **96% of their combined life savings was at 100% risk**. Remarkable!

After several meetings, I put together a plan that secured Mike and Carla's basic retirement income gap need for life. The plan even indexed their guaranteed income to a COLA of 3%, providing purchasing power protection against the effects of future inflation. All of their principal would be protected from market risk, and each of them would have a guaranteed income that neither could outlive. The plan would require Mike and Carla to take approximately $500,000 of the $838,000 currently at risk in the market and roll it over to a safe-money IRA income instrument, backed by the claims-paying ability of one of the largest and highest rated life insurance companies in the world. Their future income would be guaranteed by a multibillion-dollar company that had not broken a financial promise in its 120-plus years of existence! Mike and Carla had come to a fork in the road, and this plan would make sure their financial bridge would hold their weight as they crossed over into the golden years of retirement. Mike and Carla were happy.

As I answered Mike's phone call, I was quickly stunned. Mike was calling me to cancel our appointment—the one where we would sign the paperwork and secure his guaranteed retirement income. Why?

Mike had just finished meeting with his Wall Street financial planner, who was not at all happy with Mike's decision to withdraw *some of **his own** money* from his firm's brokerage account. After a long conversation, Mike was convinced that it was somehow *not* in his best interest to opt for guaranteed income to cover his income gap *need*. Somehow, it was not in his best interest to

guarantee that he and Carla would both be able to realize their lifelong goals during retirement, just as they had planned. Instead (surprise, surprise), his Wall Street broker's advice was that "a simple rebalancing and diversification **of risk**" was all Mike and Carla needed. The "gods" again were looking out for Mike and Carla's best interest.

Here we go opening the door to risk.

Once again, a Wall Street financial demigod was winking at risk. Not surprisingly, the broker reminded Mike and Carla that it was *his* advice that had had gotten them to this point in their financial lives. As though that indebted Mike and Carla to continue to risk *their money* (and failure) in retirement! One thing was certain: whether or not Mike and Carla make it through their retirement years without running out of income, their broker will continue to earn fees and commissions off the risk of failure they will assume. In the end, Mike decided it was in his best interest to keep 96% of his entire life savings **at risk** in the market! How long before risk would once again bite the hand that fed it?

Did Mike actually realize what he was opening the door to? Did he realize he had determined to travel several years of the final leg of life's financial journey on a perilous and narrow one-way bridge? A rickety bridge full of risk and wrought with peril? One that would allow no space for a successful U-turn, and no time for a do-over? Did Mike understand that the one-way bridge he chose was built solely upon the foundation of risk? Here is the truth: Neither he, Carla, nor their financial advisor have any clue what could be lurking in the future of financial markets over the next five, ten, twenty, or thirty years.

Maybe the financial markets will defy the uphill mathematical odds now set against them as 10,000 new baby boomers turn 65 *daily*. Why is that statistic a risk for those retiring today? Once retired, those baby boomers cease buying new stocks, bonds, and mutual funds. Worse, they begin selling them rapidly for the first time ever. What do more sellers than buyers do to any market? They cause the value of whatever they are selling to decrease.

The last baby boomer will not turn 65 until 2029.[20] At that point, it is estimated that two thirds of all baby boomers will still be alive. And they will

---

20 Pew Research Center, "Baby Boomers Retire," December 29, 2010. Accessed May 15, 2018 at http://www.pewresearch.org/fact-tank/2010/12/29/baby-boomers-retire/.

all be emptying (selling) their IRA portfolios every day in order to create income—or, in the case of those who don't need the income, in order to fulfil government-mandated Required Minimum Distributions (RMDs). Never has *any financial market* been tested in such a massive, perpetual, downward selling environment. Did Mike really understand any of this?

Who will buy the stocks Mike and all the other baby boomers will need to sell while progressing through retirement? According to a report published in August 2017, one third of millennials don't have the money to buy a house and move out of their parent's basement today, let alone buy stocks.[21] Maybe Mike and his wife Carla will always have enough buyers willing to pay a sufficiently high price for the "securities" they own in their IRA. Maybe those sales will indeed create the income they *must* have in order to live out the golden years they dream of. Maybe. Is that what Mike and Carla worked and sacrificed their whole life for—*Maybe*?

One thing is for sure: Mike, at the advice of his Wall Street financial adviser, chose to walk away from the guaranteed financial promise of a multibillion-dollar, AAA-rated financial company. One that had never missed a promised payout in over a century and a quarter of operation. Mike had been convinced that he and Carla could achieve an adequate measure of "safety" while lying in the hand of "risk"! In truth, Mike's decision guaranteed only two certainties:

1. Mike and Carla will live out their days under the constant *uncertainty* that comes with the peril of risk. There will be worry and reason for concern <u>every day of their retirement life.</u>

2. Mike and Carla have guaranteed an "annuity payment" in the form of management fees to and for their Wall Street financial adviser. He and his firm will get paid regardless of whether or not Mike and Carla make it. **His advice guaranteed protection of *his income*, while it maintained risk for *Mike and Carla's income*.**

21   Jonathan Vespa, "Jobs, Marriage and Kids Come Later in Life," August 2017. Accessed May 15, 2018 at https://www.census.gov/library/stories/2017/08/young-adults.html.

In whose financial shoes would you rather walk: Mike and Carla's, or their financial adviser's?

Everyone is wired differently. Apparently, Mike was wired to embrace the idea of chance, risk, and peril, over the idea of safety, guarantees, and peace of mind. Or maybe his broker really is a financial god and Mike has nothing to worry about!

[Quick footnote: In the 1980s, E.F. Hutton was caught up in a number of ethical and legal troubles. The largest of these was a "check kiting" scandal uncovered in 1985. Branches of the firm were caught writing checks against accounts at various regional banks, then funding those accounts with checks from yet other banks. This strategy, known as "chaining," gave Hutton the use of money in both accounts until the checks cleared.[22] In effect, the firm was giving itself an interest-free loan.[23] To make matters worse, later in early 1987, an internal Hutton probe revealed that brokers at an office in Rhode Island laundered money for the Patriarca crime family. E.F. Hutton was about to be criminally indicted.[24] This last scandal was uncovered only a week before the 1987 stock market crash (that no one saw coming). By the end of November 1987, the firm had lost $76 million, largely due to massive trading losses and margin calls that its customers could not meet. The E.F Hutton story is one of many that should give middle class savers reason to pause as they consider the advice of the Wall Street Financial Adviser Industrial Complex. Other stories include the likes of Lehman Brothers, Bear Stearns, Wachovia, Bernie Madoff ... all of whom were once considered to walk among the financial gods.]

---

22 Stephen Koepp, "Placing the Blame At E.F. Hutton," September 16, 1985. Accessed May 15, 2018 at http://content.time.com/time/magazine/article/0,9171,959840,00.html.

23 Nathaniel C. Nash, "E.F. Hutton Guilty in Bank Fraud: Penalties Could Top $10 Million," May 3, 1985. Accessed May 15, 2018 at http://content.time.com/time/magazine/article/0,9171,959840,00.html.

24 Richard Halloran, "U.S. Hints at Hutton Indictment in Money Scheme," October 11, 2007. Accessed May 15, 2018 at https://www.nytimes.com/1987/10/11/us/us-hints-at-hutton-indictment-in-money-scheme.html.

Chapter Six.

Every Market Has Its Time and Place

This will no doubt surprise my Wall Street friends, but **I do believe it is *possible* to grow wealth in the stock market**. I am not suggesting that people should never invest in securities. Neither do I believe people should never own stocks during any portion of their retirement. One would be a fool to deny the *opportunity for gain* found in the stock market, especially during the twenty-year period of 1980–2000. As mentioned before, with a buy and hold strategy, the S&P 500 averaged over 17.4% per year with dividends reinvested during that period of time. Had one retired in 1980, those twenty years would have built a heck of a financial bridge!

But the real question today, or any day one stares retirement in the face, is this: Is the **current** bridge of risk likely strong enough to carry retirees *for the next 30 years*?

As the first group of baby boomers have exited the market over the past 18 years, Wall Street risk has barely carried them along. From 2000–2017, *even after the stellar run-up of 2017*, the market has only managed a modest 5.53 percent **average** annual gain over that 18-year period.[25] (Remember how Wall Street **average** math works.) Worse, most investors spent at least fourteen of

---

25   DQYDJ, "S&P 500 Return Calculator, with Dividend Reinvestment," May 6, 2018. Accessed May 15, 2018 at https://dqydj.com/sp-500-return-calculator/.

those eighteen years making back the "old money" they had previously lost! Let me say that again. For fourteen of the last eighteen years, the average investor was underwater, had no *new* net gains, and was only making back his old money. Money he had lost! Think about it. Fourteen of eighteen years!

Here's the $64,000 question: Is *this current risk-based Wall Street bridge* sturdy enough to warrant boomers' trust through the fixed-income years of a 20–30 year retirement? To gain insight, one need only understand simple math and the power of *demographic periods of economic boom and bust*.

Speaking of those periods … in Chapter Four, we talked about the first of two elements the market needed as a catalyst for its great modern-day awakening. Do you remember it? It was the tax laws that established the 401k and IRA investment era.

But a second element was also necessary. Without this second element, the 401k and IRA tax laws would lie impotent today and remain a fading ember on the ash heap of tax law history. The 401k ember needed the gentle blowing of a sustained wind … a wind rich with the oxygen of **guaranteed mathematical people growth** … a generation of baby boomers! Timing is everything. Now you're ready to learn the rest of the truth!

Real Market Math behind the Baby Boomers

Over 10,000 baby boomers turn 65 every day. Much has been written about the economic influence this generation has wielded. However, most baby boomers don't understand how much the financial markets rise and fall with **their** buying and selling.

Think about the 10,000 baby boomers who are celebrating their 65th birthday today. What were they doing 38 years ago in 1980? Celebrating their 27th birthdays, of course! Probably by going out to dinner with friends after a solid day's work at their well-paying jobs. Many had graduated college for the first time in their family's history.

In 1980, these 10,000 people were prime candidates to invest in the stock market using the newfangled 401k strategy. You know who else were prime candidates? The 10,000 who celebrated their birthday **the next day**, *and the day after that*, and the day after that…. The baby boomers were earning good money, extra money, and were ready to spend it on stocks—10,000 more of them every day for the next twenty years!

The ember of the 401k strategies needed to be stoked. The baby boomers were not just a gentle wind blowing rich with "people oxygen"—they were a sustained whirlwind of 10,000 new potential stock buyers every day for twenty years. What will drive the price (demand) for stocks in the 20 to 30 years while baby boomers are found offsetting that demand with the unprecedented selling of these same "securities"? The extra income of their kids, one third of whom are living in their basements? Perhaps it will be all those low wage immigrants (legal or otherwise) who will buy their high-priced stocks. You do realize, in order for baby boomers to sell high for the next 30 years, *someone* has to buy high!

The Underlying Truth Driving Stock Value Prices

When I speak at financial retirement seminars, I ask my guests a simple multiple-choice question. **What drives the value of a company's stock price?** Here are the options:

    A.   Product Innovation

    B.   Lean Management

    C.   Growing, Positive Balance Sheets

    D.   Positive, Growing Profits

    E.   All of the Above

It's always interesting to moderate the public debate that inevitably follows the question. There are always a few people in the room who have paid close attention to these things over the years and feel they have a better-than-average grasp of how this stock market investing thing works. These people dive deep into wild speculation about why maybe option A, or option B, or option C, or D, is the underlying best choice. It's amazing how easy it is to get people tied up into second-guessing themselves on this one.

Finally, after the room is thoroughly divided, I throw gasoline on the fire of confusion: "Does anyone think the problem we are facing in reaching a consensus may be the possibility that **none** of these answers is the correct answer?"

The room grows quiet. People start looking at one another with that "What did he just suggest?" look. Occasionally, someone will either courageously yell, or sometimes sheepishly offer: "None of the above?"

Yep. The answer is "F. None of the above."

Options A through E show how Wall Street and its propaganda machine have brainwashed the public into believing that these factors cause stock prices to go up or down. Is this half-truth just an accident? Would the financial elite purposefully not tell us the whole story?

Back to our room of now very quiet retirees.

The truth is, now we have another problem. "None of the above" isn't really a satisfactory answer, is it? The vigorous debate over options A through E justly causes the audience to demand the right answer. Before launching into the answer, I offer one last chance for the handful of seasoned "Do It Yourself" portfolio managers sitting in the room to answer the question. But this time, a quiet humility usually gets the better of them. No one has the courage to pontificate further.

Get ready. Here comes one of the most profound truths you'll ever hear from the mouth of any financial planning or retirement planning professional:

People drive the price of stocks in the market.

You can hear the proverbial pin hit the seminar floor. The quizzical look on everyone's face is priceless. Instead of going straight to the math to prove this truth, allow me to offer two simple illustrations.

Suppose you bought a house. Ten years later, you decide to sell it because you believe the house had significantly increased in value (price) and you can make a handsome profit. You have painted the outside, added custom landscaping, upgraded the windows, bought updated appliances, and laid new carpet—all while operating on a lean budget. In a metaphorical sense, you have crossed off all of the tick points for options A through E in our stock value question. Yet, in order to profit, you still must *sell* the house! You must liquidate the asset to cash.

To *sell* the house, you need three things:

1. A **person**…

2. …with a **desire** to buy your house…

3. and enough **money** to buy it at the price you set/need.

Without any one of these three key ingredients, you can't sell the house for a profit.

Therefore, we can state unequivocally: *People*, with the money to buy your house, at the price you need them to buy, drive the selling price of your home. You need *people*! Even your home has no intrinsic cash value without *people* to buy it!

Now if you have 10 of those *people* … the selling price just went up, didn't it? If you only have one of those *people* … well, the price goes down. But understand: **nothing happens without *people*.** The more the merrier, the fewer the frettier!

It's no different with your stock.

Here's another illustration that's a bit more out there, yet nevertheless quite profound in its ability to accurately simplify and illustrate the complicated. Work with me. Let's say aliens from the planet Zentaur arrive in Earth's orbit today and decide they need planet Earth more than we humans do. The aliens use an advanced death ray gun that zeros in on human DNA to instantly wipe out all humans without destroying anything else on the planet. However, through some highly unlikely mutation of your immediate family's DNA, you find yourself immune to the alien DNA weapon. Tomorrow morning you wake up to find that you are the only human family left on planet Earth. Congratulations!

What is your stock worth now?

Think about it.

It's worthless, isn't it?

Now you own the Worth*less* IRA! All because you lack *people* to buy the risk-based equities held within it.

The truth is, *people* drive the underlying value of stock prices. The market's underlying value starts and ends with *people*. Not products. Not profit. Not technology. Not innovation. A company's stock has zero underlying intrinsic value without people. Furthermore, people only **lend** value to a company's stock. No stock ever has intrinsic or permanent value.

John Bogle, founder of Vanguard—one of the two largest 401k portfolio managers in the world—said it best during an interview with CNBC in June 2009:

> "Buying stocks or bonds is gambling. You're betting on prices—you're betting on buying them from those who don't know how much they're worth and selling them to somebody who thinks they're worth more. That's speculation, and it's short term. **It's influenced and *driven by <u>supply and demand</u>*, and not by the worth of those companies whose value lies underneath that stock price.**"[26]

Without sufficient demand (people), the price/value of all equity-based investments (securities) is nearly "Worth*less*". Now, let's apply this simple-math truth to history. Remember that 10,000 more buyers (people) entered the market *every day* for 20 years beginning in 1980. Couple that with dramatically rising incomes over the same 20-year period. Rising people… rising demand…

---

26 JeeYeon Park, "Buying Stocks or Bonds is 'Gambling': John Bogle," June 9, 2009. Accessed May 15, 2018 at https://www.cnbc.com/id/31190046. Emphasis added.

rising income… rising stock value. How much financial planning know-how would it really take to pick winning stocks over that same period of time?

Are you beginning to feel a bit misled yet?

From 1980 to 2000, the market was like a balloon with more air going in every day than air coming out. Laws of math and physics dictate that the balloon is going to get bigger, and **bigger**, and **BIGGER**! There's nothing complicated about this. Financial Advisers had nothing to do with it. A blind monkey could have picked a winning stock during that period of time, more often than not!

However, what goes up must come down. As baby boomers age and begin selling their stock—to the tune of 10,000 **new sellers** every day—what happens to the size of that balloon? Do you really want to have 96% of your life savings tied to the value of stocks, bonds, and mutual funds during a 20-year period of "air letting" deflation pressure? Where will the replacement air come from? That air is needed not just to fund baby boomers' retirements but also to keep the price value of stocks on the increase so that the following generation can also profit enough to someday retire. What happens if the X and Millennial generations (on top of not having enough *extra money* to buy stocks) decide that the stock market is not likely to provide the retirement savings and stability they desire? Today barely half of Generation X and only one third of Millennials are investing any money in the stock market.[27] Volatility and lack of investable income are at the top of their reasons for avoidance. This does not bode well for baby boomers who need these generations to buy the securities they own today in order to fund their retirement for tomorrow. Boomers will be forced to sell. Who will be forced to buy?

To ensure this unprecedented "air letting" sale of securities, the IRA laws and IRS rules demand that the balloon must deflate. What goes in must come out. At 70 ½ years of age, retirees *must* begin to sell the stocks, bonds and mutual funds in their IRA. It's the law! Like it or not. Want it or not. Need it or not. Market conditions up or down, you have to sell! Even the "income producing"

---

27 Bankrate, "Only 1 in 3 Millennials are Investing in the Stock Market." Accessed May 15, 2018 at https://www.bankrate.com/pdfs/pr/20160706-July-Money-Pulse.pdf.

bonds held in an IRA that boomers were counting on to provide long-term income throughout their retirement must be sold under IRA tax law rules.

Oops. Something else they forgot to tell you. Another *unintended* consequence!

Reality vs. The Financial "Gods"

To make matters worse for the financial "gods" who tout the wisdom of retirement risk, the days of Required Minimum Distributions (RMDs) will likely last over 30 years for many boomers as baby boomers continue to live longer! Do you think the thieving thug called risk might do a little more than knock at one's door during this unprecedented **30-year cycle of selling**? Should financial advisers really be counseling wise and prudent savers to store a majority of their retirement savings in this era of the stock market? A market saturated with risk and loaded with 10,000 new sellers every day for the next 20 years? A market which will likely be supported during that time by two generations who don't trust it, don't like risk, and don't have the high-level incomes to invest even if they did?

What happened to the power of the financial "gods" during the 2000–2002 dot-com bubble? Were they able to protect their clients' "wealth?" These "gods" looked pretty impotent, didn't they? And in mid-2007–2008? Impotent again! Yet in truth, we haven't even seen the beginning of the economic tsunami caused by the two thirds of baby boomers still headed toward the shores of our financial market's selling frenzy. What will the "gods" do then? My guess…. Tell us we're in it for the long haul, of course!

But don't worry. Remember, risk is good. You have incredibly smart "financial demigods" managing the lifeline to your retirement income and savings strategy, winking away the certain risk of this financial tsunami. And getting paid to do it, win or lose!

More than One Voice Calling out the Peril

While I'd love to take credit for being the only person to have figured all this out, I'm nowhere close. This reality has been talked about and forecast for decades. Smart people, almost from the very onset of the baby boomer driven IRA/401k stock market awakening, have been warning us. Here are a handful of headline articles and books by people who have warned us down through the years about the coming day of reckoning. You can search the internet to find them. I offer these only for those possessing the courage to consider wise counsel.

- The Ripple Effect of Baby Boomer Retirement *(US News and World Report)*
- Baby boomers' retirement: The country's biggest most predictable train wreck? *(TheMiamiHerald.com)*
- What Baby Boomers' Retirement Means For the U.S. Economy *(FiveThirtyEight.com)*
- Baby boomers are retiring — and it's going to have a huge impact on the economy *(BusinessInsider.com)*
- Shocking Baby Boomer Retirement Statistics That Keep Us Up at Night *(AGCWorldwide.com)*
- Do 10,000 baby boomers retire every day? *(Washington Post)*
- Baby boomers may be bad news for stock market *(NBCNews.com)*
- The Demographic Cliff *(Harry Dent, Harvard MBA & New York Times Best Selling Author)*

The list could literally go on and on. Yet, strangely, try to find a vaunted brokerage firm with the courage to warn their clients of the pending unprecedented economic stock sell-off by baby boomers as they navigate their retirement years. One would have better luck finding the proverbial needle in a haystack!

Think about this alarming reality. As an investor in the market, in order to win you must sell. And in order to **permanently win**, you must remove your winnings from the market. (Remember, Walmart will not cash your brokerage statement.) Conversely, Wall Street financial advisers win as long as your money is with them, in the market. The only time they **permanently lose** is when you sell your stock *and take that money out of the market*. Ironically, the only time you and I permanently win is when our broker or Wall Street adviser permanently loses. Why should we rely on retirement income planning advice from someone who permanently loses only when we permanently win? His income incentive is diametrically opposed to ours! How backward is that? Perhaps we shouldn't listen.

After all, you do want to win, don't you?

Chapter Seven.

The Post 2008 Stock Market Recovery: Real & Sustainable, or Hocus Pocus Dominocus?

Have you ever felt like someone was lying to you, but you just couldn't put your finger on the truth? Worse, how about this: You knew someone was lying to you, but you **didn't want** to put your finger on the truth!

Such were the days of the 2008 stock market recovery.

While no one would dare whisper a complaint about seeing their 401k recover back to its pre-2008 and/or pre-2000 account values, many quietly whispered, "But it just doesn't 'feel' like a recovery."

That's because it wasn't a *real* recovery. Not then, and not today.

Let's try doing something Wall Street and their Elite don't want us to do: *Think* about it! Let's apply logic and simple mathematics. Millions of people were out of work in the years following 2008. That means they had no income to buy stocks with. Of the jobs that would follow 2008 during the years of the so-called recovery, most were nowhere close to the high-paying jobs that workers lost in 2008. No one denies this fact!

Think logically now. Math is math. Do people buy stocks with "extra" income, or "less" income? So if people have *less* income after 2008—and, for almost 10 years, fewer people are employed than were employed at the market's previous all-time high—**who is buying all the stock** it would take to create a legitimate stock market recovery? Hmm? You weren't supposed to ask that question. You were just supposed to be glad your 401k value recovered!

Virtually everyone with a 401k saw it lose at least half its value in the aftermath of the 2008 crash. The underclass did not have trillions of extra seed money (cash) sitting around, available to plow back into the market and take advantage of all the new "low priced" stocks. Yet, out of *this undeniable reality*—a cash-poor, unemployed/underemployed broke population—the market began its historic and meteoric recovery, rising to new all-time new heights. Is it math being math? Or is it Hocus Pocus Dominocus math? Wall Street would have you and I believe it is math being math. Is this true? Absolutely. It all makes perfect mathematical sense! Trust us! We would never conceal the truth from you!

Really.

In addition to this remarkable economic headwind that ran against the post-2008 market, GDP grew at an eight-year average of slightly under 2%. Simultaneously, the average median wage for the *underclass* actually *decreased*. What a recovery! Surely people had TRILLIONS of extra dollars to buy stocks with during this period of time—NOT!

This is the hard economic truth.

Yet on the other hand, there was nevertheless a congruent nine-year stock market recovery of nearly 350% by the end of 2017. Exactly how does that math work? How can you do that? Where did those TRILLIONS of *extra* dollars come from? Hocus Pocus Dominocus!

In truth, you lie about how you did it.

You print money.

You deceive the mass population with a bought-and-paid-for media telling them things are wonderful.

In the meantime, you begin printing even more massive amounts of new money.

You obfuscate the truth about why you are printing this massive amount of money (public debt) through your bought-and-paid-for media.

You print more colossal amounts of new money!

You lie some more about where the colossal amount of newly printed money is really going, and for what purpose it is going there.

You allow large cap publicly traded corporations to borrow trillions of dollars, ostensibly from that newly printed money supply, because the banks were all broke after 2008—right?

You lie some more about how great the economy is and how broad the economic recovery is.

Then, after all the printing, all the obfuscation of truth, and lying, you mask the fact that corporations have taken that borrowed cash and begun a massive, unprecedented, stock-buyback binge that has lasted now nine years (and counting). In short, you enable large cap S&P 500 companies to buy back their own stock, not with cash they earned from profits, but rather with "OPM" (**O**ther **P**eople's **M**oney)—taxpayer money. Printed money. Yep. The average American bailed out the purveyors of risk and the Wall Street Elite—again!

Wash, rinse, and repeat.

Oh, and you continue to perpetuate the obfuscation of truth in order to make the general public think the whole thing is real, that there is absolutely no reason not to trust these scoundrels again into the future. After all, unemployment is down.... Corporate profits are up.... We're in a massive recovery! But, in reality, a recovery only if you owned stock, and only **if you are smart enough to sell that stock before the debt bubble bursts.**

That's how you'd do it. Is that how *they* did it?

After 2008, Central banks around the globe went into an unprecedented money-printing frenzy called "Quantitative Easing," or QE for short. Nomenclatures like QE are generally created with the intention to mask from the public what is really going on. In this case, the printing of money and the sale of your great-great-grandchildren's future through public debt. **Public debt is the welfare program which finances the lifestyle of, and perpetuates the power of, the global financial elite.**

But it's not real. Not a penny of it. And it won't last. Liars figure and figures lie. Especially on Wall Street. The stock recovery following the crash of 2008 will eventually go down in history as one of the greatest frauds Wall Street and its triad of willing accomplices—the Federal Reserve Bank, the accommodating majority of US Congress, and the elite media—ever perpetrated on the American public. I'm going to go out on a limb and predict that when this colossal debt bubble bursts, Congress will hold investigations for the next millennium (if we survive), and no one will ever go to jail. In the aftermath, who knows how we (the underclass) will ever dig out from the largest debt-financed stock and bond market bubble in world history?

Welcome to serfdom—forever!

Hidden in Plain Sight

How could such a massive financial lie go undocumented and unchallenged? Actually, it didn't go undocumented. At least not by everyone in the media. It just wasn't ever challenged on the proverbial "front page" of big media. Nevertheless, plenty of smart people have been sounding the warning blasts, pretty much all along the way. It was hidden in plain sight for those who cared to look. A simple search on Google (available until Google changes its algorithms to hide the truth) more than documents the point that the current recovery is "fake news," manufactured solely through a debt-financed corporate buyback of stock, **year after year** since 2009. Read through the following headlines and prepare to be shocked:

About 133,000,000 results (0.48 seconds)

All   News   Images   Shopping   Videos   More   Settings   Tools

There Has Been Just One Buyer Of Stocks Since The Financial Crisis ...
https://www.zerohedge.com/.../there-has-been-just-one-buyer-stocks-financial-crisis ▾
Jul 17, 2017 - "one of the major features of the US equity market **since** the low **in 2009** is that the US corporate sector has bought 18% of market cap, while ...

Who Is the WORLD'S BIGGEST Buyer of Stocks Since 2009? Hint: Not ...
https://thedailycoin.org/.../worlds-biggest-buyer-stocks-since-2009-hint-not-rothschild... ▾
Feb 26, 2018 - David Quintieri. The government structure is setup to enable corporations to lobby (bribe) our "representatives" and pass laws that are often ...

Who Is the WORLD'S BIGGEST Buyer of Stocks Since 2009? Hint: Not ...
www.investmentwatchblog.com/who-is-the-worlds-biggest-buyer-of-stocks-since-200... ▾
Feb 27, 2018 - There are two major reasons why **stocks** have risen: 1. Central banks printing money and **buying shares**. 2. **Stock** buybacks. There are two ...

The Market's Buyers And Sellers - Business Insider
www.businessinsider.com/the-markets-buyers-and-sellers-2013-5 ▾
May 21, 2013 - Companies themselves have been the biggest **buyers of stocks**. After reducing purchases during the financial crisis **in** 2008 and **2009** as ...

The biggest buyer in the market is stepping away, here's what it means ...
https://www.cnbc.com/.../the-biggest-buyer-in-the-market-is-stepping-away-heres-wha... ▾
Mar 24, 2017 - Corporate buybacks declined **in** the first quarter, but if history is any indication, ... "What's interesting is that the performance of the **stocks** with the most ... on a tear, tracking **for** the best annual performance **since 2009**, for now.

If you put $1,000 in Amazon 10 years ago, here's what you'd have now

Google

All   News   Shopping   Images   Videos   More   Settings   Tools

About 1,920,000 results (0.70 seconds)

Buffett's Berkshire Hathaway will buyback its own shares - Sep. 26, 2011
money.cnn.com/2011/09/26/markets/buffett_berkshire_buyback/index.htm ▾
Sep 26, 2011 - Warren Buffett's Berkshire Hathaway authorized **share repurchase** at up to a 10% ... By
Maureen Farrell September 26, **2011**: 11:39 AM ET.

IBM Buyback Proves Warren Buffett's Math - CNBC.com
https://www.cnbc.com/id/100690842 ▾
Apr 30, 2013 - IBM **shares** are roughly unchanged from when Buffett outlined in Berkshire's **2011**
shareholder letter why he wouldn't mind a flat **share** price ...

Netflix Earnings: Stock Buyback or Dividend? - CNBC.com
https://www.cnbc.com/id/42754971 ▾
Apr 25, 2011 - ... its **stock buyback** program, which had been on a quarter-long hiatus. ... Published 5:56
PM ET Mon, 25 April **2011** Updated 11:28 AM ET Tue, ...

5 charts show how stock repurchases boost prices - MarketWatch
https://www.marketwatch.com › Investing › Stocks › Outside the Box
Nov 18, 2014 - **Stock buybacks** among companies in the S&P 500 Index neared an ... an average of
165% since early **2011**, while **stock repurchases** over total ...

Buffett Spots Fresh Bargain: Shares in His Own Company - WSJ
https://www.wsj.com/articles/SB10001424052970204831304576594582853871222
Sep 27, 2011 - In a **share repurchase**, or buyback, a company takes some of its shares ... putting **2011**
on track to be the third-busiest buyback year on record.

Berkshire Hathaway spends $1.2B on share buyback - USA Today
https://www.usatoday.com/story/money/business/2012/12/12/...buyback/1765149/ ▾

All News Shopping Images Videos More   Settings Tools

About 3,710,000 results (0.83 seconds)

Apple Announces Plans to Initiate Dividend and Share Repurchase ...
https://www.apple.com/.../2012/.../19Apple-Announces-Plans-to-Initiate-Dividend-an... ▼
Mar 19, 2012 - CUPERTINO, California—March 19, **2012**—Apple® today announced plans to initiate a dividend and **share repurchase** program commencing ...

Apple Announces $11 Dividend And Share Buyback - Business Insider
www.businessinsider.com/apple-announces-plan-to-initiated-dividend-an-a-share-buy... ▼
Mar 19, 2012 - The **buyback** authorization is worth $10 billion and starts in fiscal 2013, which starts after September 30, **2012**. (Important note: a **buyback** ...

Stock Buybacks Are Killing the American Economy - The Atlantic
https://www.theatlantic.com/politics/archive/2015/02/kill-stock-buyback.../385259/ ▼
Feb 8, 2015 - **Stock Buybacks** Are Killing the American Economy ... work in a booth on the floor of the New York Stock Exchange on Tuesday, July 3, **2012**.

IBM Buyback Proves Warren Buffett's Math - CNBC.com
https://www.cnbc.com/id/100690842 ▼
Apr 30, 2013 - 25, **2012** shareholder letter raised some investor eyebrows. Buffett's point to investors was **share buybacks** at a reasonable price can add ...

Berkshire Hathaway spends $1.2B on share buyback - USA Today
https://www.usatoday.com/story/money/business/2012/12/12/...buyback/1765149/ ▼
Berkshire Hathaway spends $1.2B on **share buyback**. AP Published 5:25 p.m. ET Dec. 12, **2012** | Updated 5:37 p.m. ET Dec. 12, **2012**. warren buffett book party ...

Wall Street's new drug is the stock buyback - MarketWatch
https://www.marketwatch.com › Markets › U.S. & Canada › Market Extra

All   News   Shopping   Images   Videos   More   Settings   Tools

About 850,000 results (0.61 seconds)

S&P 500 Stock Buybacks Up 19% in 2013 - PR Newswire
https://www.prnewswire.com/.../sp-500-stock-buybacks-up-19-in-2013-252439381.ht... ▾
Mar 26, 2014 - NEW YORK, March 26, 2014 /PRNewswire/ -- S&P 500 **Stock Buybacks** Up 19% in **2013**.
Fourth quarter up 1% over the third quarter.

Stock buybacks beat the market - MarketWatch
https://www.marketwatch.com › Commentary › Mark Hulbert
Published: May 3, **2013** 1:49 p.m. ET. **Share** .... Past research has found **buyback stocks** continue to
outperform the market in each of the four years following the ...

S&P 500 Stock Buyback History - Business Insider
www.businessinsider.com/sp-500-stock-buyback-history-2014-4 ▾
Apr 5, 2014 - Because the S&P 500 rose 30% in **2013**, corporations actually increased the money spent
on **buybacks** by a massive amount. "S&P 500 companies repurchased $476 bn of equity in **2013**
representing 19% growth vs. 2012," said Kaiser. "We forecast nearly $600 bn of **buyback** activity in **2014**
for 23% growth this year."

McDonald's: Burgers, Fries And Stock Buybacks - Forbes
https://www.forbes.com/sites/aalsin/.../mcdonalds-burgers-fries-and-stock-buybacks/ ▾
Apr 27, 2017 - Plenty of Americans are addicted to Big Macs. McDonald's executives, on the other hand,
appear to be addicted to something equally unhealthy: **Stock buybacks**. From **2014** to 2016, McDonald's
executives spent a whopping $20.5 billion on **buybacks**.

After Forking Out $110 Billion on Stock Buybacks, IBM Shifts Its ...
https://www.fool.com/.../04/.../after-forking-out-110-billion-on-stock-buybacks-ib.asp... ▾
Apr 25, 2016 - In **2014**, after nearly three years of failure and debt-fueled **stock buybacks**, Rometty called
off the $20-per-share target. There's nothing wrong ...

All   News   Shopping   Images   Videos   More   Settings   Tools

About 943,000 results (0.64 seconds)

Buyback announcements jumped to a three-month high in July after faltering for a couple of months, and 2014 is on track to become the third-biggest year for buybacks ever, according to Minyi Chen, portfolio manager for the **AdvisorShares TrimTabs** Float Shrink ETF TTFS, +0.37% which picks stocks in part on their buyback ...   Aug 7, 2014

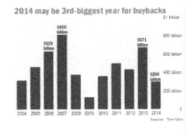

3 reasons why stock buybacks are booming - MarketWatch
https://www.marketwatch.com/.../3-reasons-why-stock-buybacks-are-booming-2014-08-...

❓ About this result   ⚑ Feedback

3 reasons why stock buybacks are booming - MarketWatch
https://www.marketwatch.com › Investing › Stocks › Market Extra
Aug 7, 2014 - Buyback announcements jumped to a three-month high in July after faltering for a couple of months, and 2014 is on track to become the third-biggest year for buybacks ever, according to Minyi Chen, portfolio manager for the **AdvisorShares TrimTabs** Float Shrink ETF TTFS, +0.37% which picks stocks in part on their buyback ...

5 biggest share buybacks of 2014 | Fortune.com
fortune.com/2014/05/29/5-biggest-share-buybacks-of-2014/ ▾
May 29, 2014 - McDonald's (mcd, -1.58%), Fortune 500), the all-American fast food Mecca, announced it would put $20 billion towards **share** repurchases and ...

Corporate America's great stock buyback binge: Will 2015 mark the ...
fortune.com › Finance › Share Buybacks ▾

stock buybacks 2015

Google

All   News   Shopping   Images   Videos   More   Settings   Tools

About 1,050,000 results (0.62 seconds)

Stock buybacks, in which companies **buy back** their own **stocks** and reduce the number of shares on the market, surged to $561 billion in **2015**—a 40% increase from the year earlier and the highest since 2007's $721 billion. And that figure is expected to rise another 7% for 2016 to $600 billion, according to Goldman Sachs. Apr 25, 2016

Stock Buybacks: What's Keeping the Market Up | Fortune
fortune.com/2016/04/25/buybacks-stock-market/

 About this result   Feedback

Stock Buybacks Are Killing the American Economy - The Atlantic
https://www.theatlantic.com/politics/archive/2015/02/kill-stock-buyback.../385259/ ▾
Feb 8, 2015 - **Stock Buybacks** Are Killing the American Economy ... Feb 8, **2015** ... 500 have spent an astounding 54 percent of profits on **stock buybacks**.

US stock buybacks are killing economic growth - CNBC.com
https://www.cnbc.com/2015/09/08/ybacks-are-killing-economic-growth.html ▾
Sep 8, 2015 - Since 2004 more than $6.9 trillion went into them, according to data compiled by Mustafa Erdem Sakinç of The Academic-Industry Research Network. According to Goldman Sachs, **stock buybacks** will surge by 18 percent in **2015**, exceeding $600 billion and accounting for nearly 30 percent of total cash spending.

Stock Buybacks: What's Keeping the Market Up | Fortune
fortune.com › Finance › stock buybacks ▾
Apr 25, 2016 - **Stock buybacks**, in which companies **buy back** their own **stocks** and reduce the number of shares on the market, surged to $561 billion in **2015**—a 40% increase from the year earlier and the

stock buybacks 2016   🎤 🔍

All   News   Shopping   Images   Videos   More   Settings   Tools

About 1,100,000 results (0.68 seconds)

Total Shareholder Returns: Silverblatt determined that total shareholder return through regular cash dividends and **buybacks** increased 13.5% to $239.1 billion for Q4 **2016**, up from $210.6 billion for Q3 **2016**. Full-year **2016** shareholder return totaled $934.6 billion, down 2.2% from $954.5 billion for 2015. Mar 22, 2017

S&P 500 Buybacks Total $135.3 Billion for Q4 2016, Decline for Full ...
https://www.prnewswire.com/.../sp-500-buybacks-total-1353-billion-for-q4-2016-declin...

                                                    ❓ About this result   🏳 Feedback

Why are stock buybacks lower in 2016? - CNBC.com
https://www.cnbc.com/2016/10/28/why-are-stock-buybacks-lower-in-2016.html ▾
Oct 28, 2016 - Google parent Alphabet announced a $7 billion **buyback** yesterday after the close. That got a lot of attention, but the **buyback** trend has been ...

20 Companies Buying Back the Most Stock in 2016 - MarketWatch
https://www.marketwatch.com › 247WallSt.com
Jun 23, 2016 - (NYSE: JPM) free to get its way on **buybacks**, at least that is the hope. CEO Jamie Dimon's crew spent $1.696 billion for **stock buybacks** in the first quarter of **2016**, for a total of $5.412 billion in its trailing 12-month period. Shares closed at $62.71, with a market cap of $230 billion.

S&P 500 Buybacks Total $135.3 Billion for Q4 2016, Decline for Full ...
https://www.prnewswire.com/.../sp-500-buybacks-total-1353-billion-for-q4-2016-decl... ▾
Mar 22, 2017 - Total Shareholder Returns: Silverblatt determined that total shareholder return through regular cash dividends and **buybacks** increased 13.5% to $239.1 billion for Q4 **2016**, up from $210.6 billion for Q3 **2016**. Full-year **2016** shareholder return totaled $934.6 billion, down 2.2% from $954.5 billion for 2015.

stock buybacks 2017

Google

All　News　Shopping　Images　Videos　More　Settings　Tools

About 1,410,000 results (0.83 seconds)

Stock Buybacks: The Greatest Deception - Forbes
https://www.forbes.com/sites/investor/2017/.../stock-buybacks-the-greatest-deception/ ▾
Jul 24, 2017 - In a company buyback, shareholders basically just get part of their own money back. It's
different than a ... **stock buybacks**, a huge crutch for stocks during this bull market, are diminishing. ...
The Toughest Jobs To Fill In **2017**.

The Ugly Truth Behind Stock Buybacks - Forbes
https://www.forbes.com/.../2017/.../shareholders-should-be-required-to-vote-on-stock-... ▾
Feb 28, 2017 - In November 2016, Goldman Sachs' chief equity strategist David Kostin estimated that, in
2017, S&P 500 companies will spend $780 billion on **buybacks** — a new record. For most of the 20th
century, **stock buybacks** were deemed illegal because they were thought to be a form of **stock** market
manipulation.

US companies spent $4T buying back their own stock - New York Post
https://nypost.com/2017/08/19/us-companies-spent-4t-buying-back-their-own-stock/ ▾
Comment(required). August 19, **2017** | 5:39pm ... The buyback binge is not isolated to market giants like
Apple, which spent $7.2 billion in the first three months of this year on **stock buybacks**. Crowd-sourcing
review site Yelp's board just ...

S&P 500 companies slash share buybacks despite record cash levels ...
https://www.marketwatch.com › Markets › U.S. & Canada › The Tell
Jun 21, 2017 - For the 12-month period ending March **2017**, S&P 500 companies spent $508.1 billion on
buybacks, down 13.8% from $589.4 billion for the prior 12-month period, which was an all-time high. In
previous years, **stock buybacks** reduced total share count, actively supporting earnings per share.

[PDF] Stock Market Indicators: S&P 500 Buybacks & Dividends
https://www.yardeni.com/pub/buybackdiv.pdf ▾
June 12, 2018 / **Stock** Market Indicators: S&P 500 **Buybacks** & Dividends ... 2006 2007 2008 2009 2010

Many forces have fueled the bull market we have witnessed over the past six years, but share repurchases are at the top of the list. Driven by low interest rates and an economy rife with uncertainty, Corporate America is awash with cash. Rather than spend that money on internal investments that might not pan out, companies have instead decided to return that money to shareholders by buying their own stock.

The debate over whether it's better for firms to send money to shareholders in the form of buybacks or in the form of dividends has gone on for decades. But we can all agree that companies ramping up their share repurchasing has buoyed stock prices. This chart from Bianco Research shows how buybacks have soared since the end of the recession and are now close to all-time highs:

There Has Been Just One Buyer Of Stocks Since The Financial Crisis

by Tyler Durden
Mon, 07/17/2017 - 18:35

0
SHARES

When discussing Blackrock's latest quarterly earnings (in which the company missed on both the top and bottom line, reporting Adj. EPS of $5.24, below the $5.40 exp), CEO Larry Fink made an interesting observation: "**While significant cash remains on the sidelines, investors have begun to put more of their assets to work**. The strength and breadth of BlackRock's platform generated a record $94 billion of long-term net inflows in the quarter, positive across all client and product types, and investment styles. The organic growth that BlackRock is experiencing is a direct result of the investments we've made over time to build our platform."

While the intention behind the statement was obvious: to pitch Blackrock's juggernaut ETF product platform which continues to steamroll over the active management community, leading to billions in fund flow from active to passive management every week, if not day, he made an interesting point: cash remains on the sidelines even with the S&P at record highs.

In fact, according to a chart from Credit Suisse, Fink may be more correct than he even knows. As CS' strategist Andrew Garthwaite writes, "**one of the major features of the US equity market since the low in 2009 is that the US corporate sector has bought 18% of market cap, while institutions have sold 7% of market cap.**"

What this means is that since the financial crisis, **there has been only one buyer of stock**: the companies themselves, who have engaged in the greatest debt-funded buyback spree in history.

Photographer: Krisztian Bocsi/Bloomberg

Technology

T-Mobile Starts $1.5 Billion Buyback After Nixed Sprint Deal

By Scott Moritz
December 6, 2017, 10:45 AM CST *Updated on December 6, 2017, 2:01 PM CST*

| how much qe has the fed done since 2008 | Google | |

All   News   Shopping   Images   Videos   More   Settings   Tools

About 2,100,000 results (0.77 seconds)

$12 trillion of QE and the lowest rates in 5,000 years ... for this?

https://www.cnbc.com/.../12-trillion-of-qe-and-the-lowest-rates-in-5000-years-for-this... ▼
Jun 13, 2016 - "The cocktail **of QE**, ZIRP and NIRP **has** been a potent one for Wall Street and the price ...
as **much** — there's reason to wonder why **the Fed** didn't end the ... damage being **done** to confidence
than there **is** positive to fundamentals by maintaining the stance. ... Correction: Lehman Brothers
collapsed **in 2008**.

The Fed launched QE nine years ago — these four charts show its ...

https://www.cnbc.com/.../the-fed-launched-qe-nine-years-ago--these-four-charts-show... ▼
Nov 25, 2017 - The Fed launched quantitative easing (QE), ultimately buying trillions of dollars of
government bonds and mortgage-backed securities. Between 2008 and 2015, the Fed's balance sheet,
its total assets, ballooned from $900 billion to **$4.5 trillion**.

Quantitative Easing In Focus: The U.S. Experience - Forbes

https://www.forbes.com/sites/.../11/.../quantitative-easing-in-focus-the-u-s-experience/ ▼
Nov 16, 2015 - **Quantitative Easing**, a rather unconventional monetary policy, **has** found ... **Many** major
central banks, such as **the Federal Reserve**, Bank **of** ... **In 2008**, the world faced its worst economic

ECONOMIC BEAT

Stock Buybacks Are Driving Companies Into Debt

By David Ader • August 6, 2016

Figure 63: The corporate sector has been the main buyer of US equities since the market low

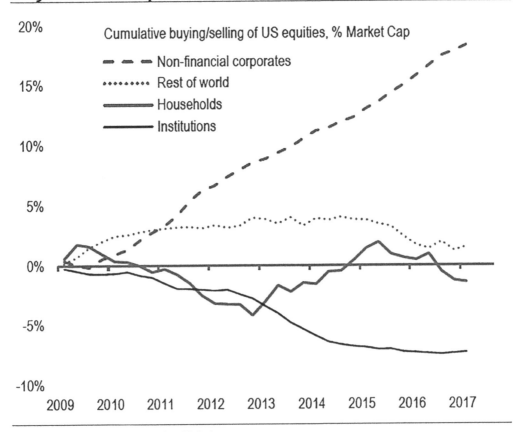

Cumulative buying/selling of US equities, % Market Cap

- - - Non-financial corporates
·········· Rest of world
======= Households
——— Institutions

Source: Thomson Reuters. Credit Suisse

One could go on, but I think you get the point. This was a massive fraud committed right out in the open. All of it in bright, high-noon daylight. Neither the financial elite of Wall Street, nor the congressional elite in Washington DC, nor our major media elite bothered to stop the insanity or tell the truth. All that mattered was masking the truth. And what is that truth? **Your 401k values and retirement future are in a world of trouble. Sustained momentarily on the foundation of massive amounts of borrowed money.**

This manufactured debt bubble is far worse than any historic criminal Ponzi scheme ever dreamt of becoming. What drove the 2008 stock market recovery? Debt. A multi-trillion-dollar mountain of borrowed money from start to finish! That's trillion with a "T"! $1,000,000,000,000.

For each one trillion dollars printed and borrowed, if you stacked each dollar on top of the other, the stack would reach a quarter of the way to the moon. After 8 trillion, you'd have a high enough mountain to reach the moon and back![28] A *mountain of debt* is a terribly understated truth.

For the last decade (at taxpayers' expense), this mountain of borrowed money has been leveraged by major large cap public stock corporations to buy back their own stock, which artificially drove up the value of your 401k.

It's not that companies didn't earn profits during those years—they did. They just didn't use those profits to buy back their stock. For the most part, those profits are still sitting on their balance sheets. The headline in the Bloomberg business article below says it all.

≡ Menu   Q Search   **Bloomberg**

Business

S&P 500 Companies Spend Almost All Profits on Buybacks

Lu Wang and Callie Bost
October 5, 2014, 11:00 PM CDT *Updated on October 6, 2014, 9:04 AM CDT*

---

28 The Endowment for Human Development, "Grasping Large Numbers." Accessed May 15, 2018 at http://www.ehd.org/science_technology_largenumbers.php.

Make no mistake, they didn't take those "record profits" and use them to buy their own stock back. No sir. First, they used borrowed funds, bailouts ultimately printed at the Federal Reserve. While you and I couldn't get a business loan, car loan, or home loan, trillions of newly printed dollars found its way to large cap S&P 500 publicly traded companies. Those companies bought back their stock with it. Then, after corporations had essentially leverage all of QE1, QE2, QE3, QE4 to buy back their stock, stocks began to run sideways for an 18-month period from the end of 2014 through the end of 2016. See chart and timeline below:

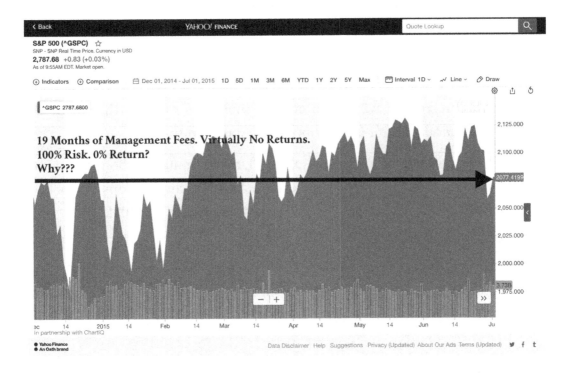

Once the Fed's cheap money supply was "downsized" at the end of 2014, you can see the market flatten out for over a year and a half. Now Wall Street had to turn to a different smoke and mirror scheme to continue the con of the ever-increasing value of their corporate stock. And what was the next scheme? Public marketed corporate bond funds. Another debt instrument!

"You baby boomers don't want our risky stocks? How about our *safe* bonds? (Bonds are not safe, but Wall Street is allowed to label them as "fixed income" or "guaranteed income" investment instruments. Placing the words "fixed" and "guaranteed" into the name of a securities instrument? Isn't that about as misleading it could possibly be? Knowing boomers were not inclined to buy their risky stocks again, corporations made the pitch: "Surely buying our bonds is much better than keeping all that money you've just received (*from our six-year-long corporate stock buyback binge*) in the bank at nearly zero point something."

And so buy we did! But understand this clearly. When a corporation sells its bonds, it is borrowing from you, me, and our neighbors. This borrowing from the public through the sale of their corporate bonds only added even *more debt* to their corporate balance sheets! Trillions of dollars of more debt! But it did give them an immediate *new supply* of trillions of dollars in cash. What did they do with this new supply of trillions in cash? They resumed their binge of stock buybacks, of course! The markets zoom upward again in 2017. All of this upon massive amounts of borrowed money. Trillions and trillions of dollars of borrowed money that you, I, and our children's children will get stuck paying back. Only we will pay it back out of our *very real* hard-earned incomes in the form of higher taxes and inflation. You and I will not get a bailout when the day of reckoning comes.

America's **government** and America's **corporations** are drowning in **debt**. This is not speculation or doomsday wolf-crying. See for yourself in the many articles posted below available to anyone who cares to ask the right questions in a simple Google search:

The conclusion: None of this *stock market recovery* has been real. And by "real," I mean a recovery fueled by money produced through real supply and demand. I mean real economic growth, represented by actual growing incomes of working Americans through real employment and the surplus savings that a high-wage job creates. Today, some people may have been re-employed, but they are buying less stock, on less income—if they are buying stock at all! Because they have *less* spendable (extra) income! Real people, buy real stocks, <u>with real "extra income."</u>

The stock market recovery may not be real, but what *is* real is that millions of baby boomers regained trust in the financial elite on Wall Street, and especially trust in their stock brokers. Collectively, we bought into the promise of risk, all over again. Wash, rinse, and repeat!

All   News   Images   Videos   Shopping   More   Settings   Tools

About 384,000 results (0.65 seconds)

S&P Warns High Corporate Debt Could Trigger Next Default Cycle ...
https://www.bloomberg.com/.../s-p-warns-high-corporate-debt-could-trigger-next-def... ▼
Feb 4, 2018 - The number of defaults by heavily indebted corporates could rise significantly amid tightening credit conditions, according to **S&P** Global Ratings. ... Removing the "easy money punch bowl" could trigger the next default cycle since high corporate **debt** levels have increased the ...

Companies 'drowning in debt' despite almost $2 trillion in ... - CNBC.com
https://www.cnbc.com/.../companies-drowning-in-debt-despite-almost-2-trillion-in-cas... ▼
May 23, 2016 - Companies '**drowning in debt**' despite almost $2 trillion in cash ... sheets, according to a study released Monday by **S&P** Global Ratings.

Americans are drowning in debt. Here's where they have it the worst ...
https://www.washingtonpost.com/.../americans-are-drowning-in-debt-heres-where-they-... ▼
Dec 8, 2017 - Rates of past-due **debt** are generally highest in southern and western states and lowest in the upper Midwest.

Corporate America Is Drowning in Debt - Fortune
fortune.com › Finance › Fortune 500 ▼
May 20, 2016 - A new report from **S&P** Global Ratings raises red flags about corporate **debt**.

Many firms with heavy load of debt face trouble - The Blade
www.toledoblade.com/.../09/.../Many-firms-with-heavy-load-of-debt-face-trouble.htm... ▼
Sep 18, 2016 - In March, 2016, **S&P** cut its ratings on Macy's to BBB, two notches above junk. ASSOCIATED ... "They're actually **drowning in debt**." It turns out ...

The Western World Is Drowning In Debt! - ChartYourTrade.com
https://chartyourtrade.com/the-western-world-is-drowning-in-debt/ ▼

All   News   Images   Videos   Shopping   More   Settings   Tools

About 21 results (0.65 seconds)

Why Is The Dow Soaring While Its Companies Are Losing Revenue?

thefederalist.com/2017/03/14/dow-soaring-companies-losing-revenue/ ▾

Mar 14, 2017 - Dating back to 1896, the Dow, which is short for **Dow Jones** ... When these 30 **corporations** do well, their share prices rise and the Dow's point value increases ... Net income fared worse, **sinking** 14.10 percent. ... Not Wall Street, which is only too happy to pick up fees for facilitating the issuance of more **debt**.

Drowning In Debt - SPDR Dow Jones Industrial Average ETF ...

https://seekingalpha.com/article/4003754-drowning-debt ▾

Sep 2, 2016 - Issuing corporate debt rather than equity has never been so attractive. ... is a reduction in the cost of borrowing for "investment grade" **corporations**. ... Perhaps I am being unfair, but, in a world which is **drowning in debt**, central ...

These companies need to worry about rising borrowing costs

money.cnn.com/2018/04/03/investing/stocks-debt-borrowing-costs.../index.html ▾

Apr 3, 2018 - **Dow** falls 459 points as trade war fears rise ... Shares of S&P 500 **companies** with at least 5% of their **debt** in floating rate bonds dropped 4% ...

Missing: ~~drowning~~

After the Bell: Dow Soars 300 Points as Utilities Lead Stocks Higher ...

https://www.barrons.com/.../after-the-bell-dow-soars-300-points-as-utilities-lead-stocks-h...

Feb 15, 2018 - The S&P 500 gained 1.2% to 2731.20 today, while the **Dow Jones** ... equally attractive, and **companies** weren't **drowning in debt**," Wilbur writes.

Cramer on the Dow Jones' 10 biggest sell-off losers - CNBC.com

https://www.cnbc.com/2018/.../cramer-on-the-dow-jones-10-biggest-sell-off-losers.ht... ▾

Feb 9, 2018 - Jim Cramer finds bull and bear cases in the **Dow Jones** industrial average's ... seen as a **sinking** ship rife with **debt** and discombobulated businesses, ... "I think the world of the **company**, but

[Note: According to Arne Alsin, "For most of the 20th century, stock buybacks were deemed illegal because they were thought to be a form of stock market manipulation. But since 1982, when they were essentially legalized by the SEC, buybacks have become perhaps the most popular financial engineering tool in the C-Suite executive management's tool shed. And it's obvious why Wall Street loves them: Buying back company stock can inflate a company's share price and boost its earnings per share—metrics that often guide lucrative executive bonuses."[29]]

Beating the Elite at Their Own Game

However, there is a way to make the stock market recovery real for your retirement. Would you like to know how to do this? It's simple. This time, sell while it's high, baby! Get out *before* the bubble bursts! Wouldn't it be tremendous if those of us in the underclass beat the elite at their own game, just once? Imagine if millions of us "regular folk" could somehow coordinate and communicate a massive sell-off, timed together so that we all sold while the market was at an all-time high. Imagine if this time, it was the middle class (underclass to the Elite) who cashed in on all the borrowed money first! Leaving the Elite with devastated balances on their monthly stock portfolio statement!

But that wouldn't be good for Wall Street. And it certainly wouldn't be good for their controlled sales representative—the financial adviser. Maybe that's why virtually no one on that side of the financial planning fence is giving the underclass that sagacious advice today!

---

29 Arne Alsin, "The Ugly Truth Behind Stock Buybacks," February 2018, 2017. Accessed May 15, 2018 at https://www.forbes.com/sites/aalsin/2017/02/28/shareholders-should-be-required-to-vote-on-stock-buybacks/#27db56356b1e.

Chapter Eight.

Wall Street Diversification = The Obfuscation of Risk

Sometimes I think people misunderstand how Wall Street brokerage firms make money. Honestly, I bet if you asked the average person on the street that question, they'd answer, "By investing in stocks."

Wrong. That's not how it works. Not even close.

Understand this: These firms don't invest *their* money. They invest *your* money. These advisory firms make money **solely on the fees and commissions** which they charge you and me to invest our money. Follow me here.

If we don't invest our money, they don't get paid fees or commissions. If they don't get paid fees and commissions, they don't make money. To make money, these firms must have **other people** give them money. Then they must charge those people fees and get paid commissions for placing **other people's money** at risk in the stock market!

The last time I looked, not a single investment advisory firm was chartered as a benevolent non-profit 501c3! Nope. Not one. They are all in business for one purpose, and one purpose only: to make money for themselves. Nothing is wrong with that. It's how businesses operate. But investors need to be aware that this is how the game is played. It also might be a reason why Wall Street advisory firms rarely want us to sell off our portfolio and take our profits out of the market—even when the market is at an all-time high. What happened to buy low and sell high?

Think about it. When did you ever get a call advising you that it was a good time to sell **and make that profit real (permanent) by taking your money out of the market because the market was at an all-time high**? Aren't we supposed to buy low and sell high? From a broker's perspective, it's fine to sell this stock *and then buy the next stock*. They'll recommend that transaction all day, every day, and twice on Sunday. Here's how the call goes. "Hey Joe, I think the ABC stock, now that it's at an all-time high, might be a good one to sell *so we can reinvest* those profits into the XYZ stock that we feel is undervalued and positioned for more growth."

Sure, *that* call you absolutely get. A thousand times you get that call. But might the reason you get that call involve the fact that **the broker makes even more money when you follow this call's advice**? After all, there's another commission for him when he makes that call, because you bought another stock! Sometimes, even a commission on both ends—the stock fund you're selling, and the one you're about to buy. Nice gig if you can get it, huh? Plus, because your money is still in the market, those management fees keep coming in month after month. That call has no risk to him. His base income is completed preserved, and even given the chance for increase. Why not make that call, if you are him?

Now look, I'm not suggesting that's the sole reason you get that call from your broker. To be clear, in most cases there is *nothing* wrong with this call. In fact, oftentimes it is exactly the kind of call you are paying him to make! But you should also keep in mind one very important thing, especially as you are about to enter or enjoy retirement: **You don't make money until you sell, and you don't get to keep (or spend) that money until you take it out of the market.** You have to withdraw it to spend it. Then, and only then, have **you** permanently won. Your broker has permanently lost.

Realize that Wall Street advisers lose when clients permanently win. Might this be why advisers generally counsel their clients to hang on to their stock portfolio and remain exposed to risk, from cradle to grave? They generally advise clients to hang on and hope for more growth in the future. In their eyes, the market is always going higher. Now, there's nothing wrong with "hoping" for our future. But there's also nothing wrong with "having" for our future. Most would agree that **having** is better than **hoping.** Given the choice, would you prefer a strategy of "have" or "hope" for your retirement future? Wall Street advises us to hope!

It is amazing to me that more people (especially those within 5 years of retirement) don't insist on removing at least half of their life savings from the risky stock market and diversifying it *from risk.* After all, that is the only way to ensure it will actually be there when they need it. Where retirement income is concerned, **to *have* is always better than to *hope*!**

The Circus Act of Rebalancing Diversification of Risk

"But my financial adviser says I'm already fully diversified! He says I have nothing significant to worry about. In fact, we just met, and he rebalanced my portfolio so that everything matches up with my age and retirement goals."

I can't tell you how often I've heard this statement. Of course your financial adviser has you "fully diversified" according to age and goals. While this Wall Street "diversification" strategy is intended to give the investor a level of confidence about one's exposure to individual stock investment risk, the truth is it does absolutely nothing to protect one's account from systemic market investment risk. Are we to believe that prior to 2008, financial advisers didn't meet with their clients every year to properly balance and fully "diversify" their portfolios to protect them from risk? If so, then why did millions of people (in their 60s and 70s, 80s and 90s!) still lose half of their life savings in 2008? Because Wall Street's definition of "diversification" simply means that when the market crash comes, you're going to lose money in a hundred different places instead of just ten. Well … isn't that what happened in 2008?

Bonds are Not Safe Diversification

Let me explain why I find the idea of a bond strategy as a "safely diversified" strategic concept so laughable. A tragic real-world story illustrates the absurdity of this obfuscation of truth.

One lady expressed concern over the security of her principal and her income to her financial advisor. So he recommended that she diversify $70,000 of her stock portfolio into corporate bonds after she retired in 2000. She didn't have a lot. This was the advisor's best tactic to protect her principal. "Let's 'diversify' into some income-producing bonds." Sounds safe, right?

U.S. | World | Politics | Money | Opinion | Health | Entertainment | Tech | Style | Travel

June 1st, 2009
09:19 AM ET

Bondholder furious over GM bankruptcy

GM bondholder Debra June speaks to CNN's John Roberts.

General Motors turns to bankruptcy today in the hopes of finding a new start. The move comes after a majority of those holding $27 billion in GM bonds agreed to swap that debt for a stake in the new General Motors.

Debra June is a small bondholder who six years ago invested $70,000 in GM bonds. She predicts that investment is now worth less than $200. She spoke to John Roberts on CNN's "American Morning" Monday.

Eight years later, in 2008, *General Motors* went bankrupt. Her $70,000 "safely diversified" bond holding was worth about $200.[30]

The truth? Corporate bonds are not safe money. It says right on the investment prospectus they force you to sign: you can lose some or all of your principal! Your financial advisor will make you sign a piece of paper before you invest in that bond saying that you have read and understand this fact.

Let me ask you something. Let's bring this whole thing home. How many reading this book lost upwards of 50% of your 401k in 2008? Many 401k/IRA holders, if honest when asked this question, would have to raise a hand in the positive. But wait. How could that be? According to our broker, didn't we have a properly balanced and fully diversified portfolio then?

See, here's the problem. Wall Street's definition of *diversification* means spreading your money across 100 different accounts: mid cap, high cap, low cap, no cap, stocks, bonds and mutual funds. All of which have risk. You are fully diversified! Whew. Don't you feel better? Now when the market crashes, you will … uh … lose money in 100 different accounts instead of 1. This is the undeniable historical result of Wall Street diversification—because it happened!

What most people need as they near and enter retirement is ***true diversification***. True diversification is putting some of one's money where it can never decrease, never be lost, and never run out. That's true diversification. But this is not the kind of diversification recommended by Wall Street.

Here's another way of saying this:

What most people need is **diversification FROM risk.** Not diversification OF risk. There is a big difference between the two. But unfortunately, Wall Street rarely sells true diversification, diversification "from risk." True diversification is what this book is all about: The value of true diversification "from risk" as a part of one's retirement income strategy!

How much ***true diversification*** is in your retirement portfolio today?

---

30 CNN, "Bondholder Furious over GM Bankruptcy," June 1, 2009. Accessed May 15, 2018 at http://am.blogs.cnn.com/2009/06/01/bondholder-furious-over-gm-bankruptcy/.

Part III.

Understanding the 401k / IRA Time
Bomb: How to Successfully Leverage
and Defuse Them

Chapter Nine.

The IRA: A Tax Savings Benefit, or a Ticking Time Bomb?

You're probably not going to like this.

You probably think your IRA is an "**I**ndividual **R**etirement **A**ccount." Would you be surprised to learn that this is just another fable the Wall Street Financial Planning Industrial Complex has planted in the mind of the underclass with its accomplices in the Federal Government and Elite Media? Yep! See the post of the actual IRS documentation taken from its official website and shown on the next page that provides it.

Okay. But that's not really such a big deal, is it? Arrangement, account, agreement ... what's the difference? Surely it's just an innocent misunderstanding. It's just a misstatement someone made that eventually caught on. Right?

Okay. Once again, let's *think* this through.

First, where the IRS is concerned, there are no "innocent mistakes". If you think otherwise, it's only because you've never been audited by the IRS. The IRS doesn't say (or do) anything by accident, let alone casually write something into official IRS code documents. If the law and code was written to say "arrangement," you can count on the fact that the word "arrangement" was carefully chosen.

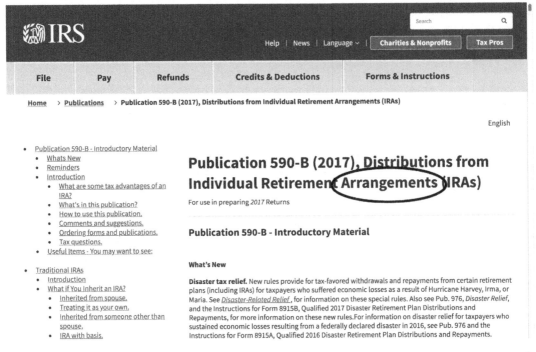

So the question becomes: Why would the IRS choose to label this "account" as an "arrangement," instead of an "agreement," or simply an "account"? What is the difference between an "account," an "agreement," and an "arrangement"?

Account vs. Agreement

Fundamentally, an account is something you can legally own. An arrangement, interestingly, is not something you can legally own. You *can* own an account outright. I own my individual bank account outright. No one else has a claim to my account. An account is something you can own. Arrangements are not something you own. Rather, one makes (or enters into) an arrangement—*with* someone else!

From the IRS's point of view, we don't **own** an individual retirement "account". We've entered into an individual retirement "arrangement". But in that context, one would think even the word "agreement" would have been a more natural choice. Yet it was not the word chosen.

Like the word "account," the word "agreement" can be very narrowly and specifically defined. As in, "**This** is what we agreed to." You can hold someone accountable to the specific terms of an agreement. An arrangement, on the other hand, carries with it a much looser connotation in terms of a "range" of definitive, accountable boundaries. For example:

"I will *arrange* your pick up at 11:00 am" is not the same as "I *agree* to pick you up at 11:00 am."

Admittedly, the casual observer might confuse them as *essentially* the same. But from a legal standpoint, the two statements are very different in terms of the responsibility they assign.

Arrangements are far vaguer than agreements. Uncle Sam and the IRS chose to use the vaguer word "arrangement" rather than the more definitive words "agreement" or "account". Interesting, don't you think?

Let's take a close look at what Wall Street and Uncle Sam have actually cooked up together with the IRA. When you carefully analyze what the IRS code actually *states*, versus what the average person generally *hears*, you quickly understand that the two are as far apart as the statements "I will arrange to pick you up" and "I will pick you up." Let's first consider what the average person hears—what the public believes.

If you've contributed to an IRA, you probably thought you were getting a tax benefit that you could leverage in the future to pay fewer taxes on the money you made in the past. The logic behind this reasoning, as explained by the sellers of this concept—Wall Street financial planners—goes something like this:

"You don't like paying taxes, do you? Let me show you how you can significantly reduce your taxable burden today. We'll shift a portion of your income into an IRA which will not be taxed today. It'll be taxed in the future, once you've retired. Because your income will be much lower during retirement, you will be in a lower tax bracket, and thus have to pay less money to the government on that income. You do plan to make more money now while you're working than when you're retired, right? But wait, it even gets better. This strategy will permit growth on the dollars that you accumulate over the years, without having to pay any tax until you begin to take the money out as income once you've entered retirement. You'll save money now (no taxes), accumulate more money for the future (increasing compound growth), then pay fewer taxes on it in the future! You can't lose! You'd be crazy not to do this. And just to prove how good it really is, guess what? They limit how much you can contribute to the IRA every year. You know it's got to be a good thing when they start putting put limits on it! What's even better is that the government offers a special IRA for your employer, called a 401k. It's basically the same thing as an IRA, only it has higher contribution limits. If you work for an employer, you can actually have both! An IRA and a 401k! But get this: your employer can match every dollar you put in the 401k up to a certain percent, according to the plan limits. You'll be passing up free money if you don't do this. What kind of person would pass up free money? If I were you, I'd be taking advantage of this IRA/401k thing before they sober up and change their mind!"

That's what we all heard in a nutshell. Yes, or no?

Expectation vs. Reality

Everything implied in that explanation is what people *expect* to have happen in the future when they contribute to an IRA or 401k. However, not everything *implied* in the explanation (sales pitch) is what the IRS's code actually states *will happen* in the future.

Implied is the idea that, in the day you finally take the income out, you will pay a lower percentage of tax on the accumulated savings amount. But is that really what the code states? If so, that would be an "agreement". One which contained a hard, fast, measurable obligation. But in reality, the IRS has never "agreed" to anything like that.

Think about it this way.

My friend Mark comes to me and says, "Jeff, I need a loan for a million dollars." And I said, "No problem, Mark. I have an extra million dollars I don't need today. I'll loan it to you. Just sign here on the dotted line and the money is yours."

What important factor is Mark going to look for before signing that loan document? The interest rate and terms of repayment, right? No one in their right mind would enter into a loan "agreement" without knowing how, and at what cost, the loan was going to be paid back. Imagine the concern my friend Mark would have if he began searching for such terms, only to find that nothing in the document I handed him stated what level of interest I would charge. Furthermore, nothing I handed him stated what size the payments would be once Mark started paying back the loan. Should Mark sign the loan document?

Would you sign that loan document?

Not on your life! No one in their right mind would sign that loan document. No attorney would allow a client to sign such a document.

Mark wisely looks at me and says, "Jeff, I know you're only trying to help me, and you have only my best interest in mind, but I have to ask: What interest rate are you going to charge me? And how large will my payments be when I have to pay this loan back?"

I reply, "Look, Mark, I don't need the money now, but I will at some point in the future. Let's just do this. When we get to the future, I'll consider my situation and decide what I need. Then I will tell you the interest rate, the payment size, and how fast you'll need to pay me back."

Again, would you sign that loan *"arrangement"*? Neither will my friend Mark!

Honestly, would you even think about offering a friend that kind of "arrangement"? Seriously, would you? Because I wouldn't! I couldn't! Truthfully, I would be hard pressed to have that conversation with my *enemy*, let alone my friend! In fact, if you came to me with that kind of offer, you would have to be an awfully good friend for me not to be tempted to punch you in the nose! What kind of dark heart does it take to have the audacity to suggest such a ridiculous and predatory "arrangement"?

Apparently, the heart of a Wall Street investment banker and the government he's in collusion with. Isn't that exactly what we have when we voluntarily fund an IRA or 401k? Where in this "arrangement" does the IRS commit to any guarantee that we will pay a lower tax rate in the future? Nowhere. Have taxes ever gone up in our nation's past? Absolutely. What are the chances they will go up in the future?

- How many times has Congress increased the Social Security payroll tax, increased or added marginal tax rates, eliminated tax deductions, etc.?

- Who will pay for the two thirds of baby boomers who are not yet drawing Social Security or Medicare benefits?

- Who will pay the federal and state pension payments for the two thirds of baby boomers who have yet to retire?

- How many of these federal programs and pensions are already broke and/or significantly underfunded today?

- Who's going to pay down our nation's 21-trillion-dollar debt? Where and from whom will that money come?

And we're supposed to believe we'll pay lower taxes on our future IRA distributions. Really? Then let's see that in writing!

But it's not in writing. In fact, we have been led into an "arrangement" with the IRS and Wall Street that:

1. Gives Wall Street the use of our money.

2. Penalizes us if we decided to take some, part, or all of it back before turning 59 ½.

3. Pledges that we will pay Uncle Sam **whatever** tax rate Uncle Sam decides he needs in the future.

4. Gives Uncle Sam the right to increase not only his percent of ownership of our account value in the future (i.e. tax rate), but also how much we must withdraw each year (RMDs).

Remember, in a marginal tax structure, this factor (RMDs) also directly affects what percentage of income one must pay Uncle Sam each year. Uncle Sam can raise tax rates *and raise RMDs*. Nothing in the arrangement Wall Street and Uncle Sam invented gives the tax payer a guarantee or limits, in any way, what can be "amended" in the future by Uncle Sam and to Uncle Sam's benefit.

Look, one could argue that none of this was what Wall Street and Uncle Sam intended as they wrote the laws and codes that govern the modern 401k/IRA tax laws. Fine, if that makes you feel better. It doesn't change the material facts of the "arrangement." Or the risk you and I assume when we volunteer to fund that perilous "arrangement."

It is a perilous arrangement because you and I actually have no clue what its value is in the end. The arrangement is that you are giving Uncle Sam a blank check to cash for whatever amount he thinks he needs in the future—and the authority to throw you in jail if the check bounces! That's what an IRA is—legally!

I told you that you weren't going to like this!

Chapter Ten.

IRA Rules, Strings, and Golden Handcuffs: Resistance is Futile!

As bad as the news in Chapter Nine was for most of us, I have more news you're not going to like. This is equally terrible news. But, like the awful news of Chapter Nine, this news is spun to make us think *positively* about Wall Street's IRA retirement strategy and *negatively* about any alternative retirement saving strategy.

A Web of Complication

IRAs are complicated because of all the financial strings attached to them. A picture of the stringed tentacles in an IRA might closely resemble the intricate trappings and complexities of a spider's web. No small living thing escapes! And what are we told about these retirement instruments? To employ a pun, each string is supposedly 'spun' to our benefit. But let's take a look at a few of the more understandable strings. Then you can decide for yourself just how beneficial this instrument is—and who might actually benefit the most.

The first string is a requirement that (with few exceptions) forces IRA holders to invest in a **securities-based** financial product—a product of **risk.** If you don't believe this, try directing your 401k contribution to something safe. Something with no market risk. Something that offers a guaranteed value or guaranteed future benefit. For the vast majority of us, those options do not exist.

Why not? After all, retirement is a critical and certain need. Wouldn't it be more logical and responsible for everyone to be able to invest a portion of his cumulative life savings into an instrument offering certainty? Why not allow—better yet, why not mandate—these retirement IRA savings instruments to include a variety of safe money financial products? (Remember, prior to the advent of the IRA, these safe money products had been used for decades by American companies and individuals to prepare for their financial futures.) Why not?

"Because." That's why!

"Besides, why would you want the option to invest in something safe for your future? What kind of idiot thinks like that? After all, you want to be rich when you retire, don't you? Only the stock market can make you rich when you retire. Everyone knows that. Without risk, there is no reward! Therefore, because we care so much about you, we're going to make it almost impossible for you to make the *mistake* of saving for your future in a place that 'limits' what you can earn. You don't want limits, do you?"

Does anyone else see the ludicrous nature of this line of reasoning?

[Note: In 1980, when 401ks were still in their infancy, you could invest in a 10-year treasury bond at a guaranteed 15% compound interest rate. Even passbook savings accounts could be found at 6% or more! Try funding your 401k into a bank savings account at 6% today. Yet safe, guaranteed, reasonable-interest-rate investment options were not included in the vast majority of 401k plans. Why not?]

Only What's Best for You

Here is the second string: Wall Street and Uncle Sam so much want you to retire with a mountain of savings, that IRA code rules prohibit you from taking your money out of an IRA until you reach age 59 ½. Or at least that's what they tell us. Once you add the money into the IRA, it's stuck there, apart from a few exceptions (all of which are complicated, require precise paperwork, and need IRS approval). If you take money out of this *arrangement* prior to age 59 ½, the IRS tacks on a 10% penalty—not to mention the marginal tax rate increase your withdraw might cause in the year you remove the funds.

"Wait. You mean I have to pay a penalty to get *my* money out if I decide I need or want it prior to age 59 ½? Why would you do that?"

"For your own good, of course! You see, this is for your retirement. If we don't put this rule in, we know you'll rob from yourself throughout your life and then have nothing saved for when you retire. This is for your own good!"

"Are you sure this is not just about putting a penalty in place so you can protect the interests of your elite friends on Wall Street and stuff your own pocket, Mr. IRS Man?"

"No, no, no. How could you possibly think such a thing? This is strictly for your own good—because we love you and are trying to ensure you succeed!"

Excuse me while I run to the bathroom.

Studies by Fidelity and Vanguard (the two largest 401k and IRA providers in the country) have indicated that more than 40% of people who have these "arrangements" end up taking withdrawals prior to age 59 ½. They pay the 10% penalty to Uncle Sam. One begins to wonder if Uncle Sam might have seen that probability coming when he wrote the penalty into the IRA tax code. As President Ronald Reagan once quipped, the nine scariest words in the English language are "I'm with the government and I'm here to help!" Whatever the underlying motive for this rule, it has a chilling effect on 401k and IRA owners, decreasing their desire to ever take a substantial withdrawal of cash out of this "arrangement"—**even after retirement!** For most, the end result is a lifetime of perpetual risk, peril, danger, and chance of loss, from cradle to grave. Whether stock values rise or fall, the only guaranteed beneficiary of such an arrangement is Uncle Sam and the financial elite of Wall Street.

Income, Or Not — It's Not Up to You

String number three has three tiers to it. Here's the first: IRA rules restrict your activity on not only the front end but also the back end. The key back-end requirement is the "70 ½ rule." Basically, this rule allows the government to force you into taking what are called RMDs (**R**equired **M**inimum **D**istributions).

To be fair, Uncle Sam has never received tax revenue from this money. The IRA never promised a tax-free benefit to a traditional IRA or 401k. Only a tax-deferred *potential* benefit. The truth is that even a Roth IRA is not tax free. Taxes are simply paid on the front end instead of the back end.

If the financial elite are so intent upon ensuring our retirement success, shouldn't we expect sage wisdom, fiduciary council, and advice from their highly trained (conditioned) financial advisory representatives? Why is it, then, that over 90% of Americans have chosen traditional IRA and 401k strategies over Roth strategies? Maybe this story will make it clear.

Say you are a farmer. The IRS man comes by and offers you two taxation options.

- Option one: You pay taxes each year on the value of the *seed* at the time you plant it in the spring.

- Option two: You pay taxes on the value of the *harvest* at the time you reap in the fall.

You quickly calculate that the value of the seed is far less than the value of the harvest. Therefore, you choose to pay taxes on the value of the seed, not the harvest.

And yet financial advisers recommend traditional IRAs and 401ks for their clients, essentially forcing the client to pay taxes on the value of the harvest instead of the seed. Who really wins? Uncle Sam, and of course, Wall Street! Not you and me.

Let me be clear. Taxes at the end of a traditional IRA are completely legitimate. However, it doesn't change the fact that we give up far more control of our money than one might think. Giving up that control can severely hurt (or possibly destroy) our financial future if taxes are pressured upward in the future.

Suppose you reach the age of 70 ½ and you don't need any income from the IRA. Suppose you want to leave what you have saved as an inheritance. It doesn't matter. You have to take it (the RMD) regardless of whether you need it or want it. Additionally, suppose the market was in a free fall, down 50% that year. Ouch! If you didn't need or want the money, would you voluntarily take it out while the market was worth 50 cents on the dollar? Absolutely not! Yet the authors of the IRA regulations included a rule forcing you to do exactly that. You must take the withdrawals, even during a down market, even if you do not need or want the income. Who is really in control of *your* money? Withdrawing money during a down market could bring a person closer to running out of money much quicker than they would like. An "unintended consequence" for sure! But a consequential one, none the less.

When, How, and at What Rate

Here is the second tier. In an IRA, you lose control of not only *when* you can withdraw money without penalty but also *how much* you have to withdraw and *at what rate*. Today the rate begins at roughly 3.6%. It increases as a person continues to grow older. The older one gets, the more one must withdraw.

But again, Uncle Sam dictates not just *when* but *how much* you must spend (draw out of your retirement nest egg). The IRA kind of sounds like your retirement marriage partner. As in any marriage, you can always say no to your partner. But we all know that that's not always a great idea. There can often be hell to pay for telling a spouse "no" at the wrong time! And if you say "no" to Uncle Sam at the age of 70 ½ during your retirement "marriage, *hell* "charges you a whopping 50% penalty on whatever amount of the RMD you declined. Of course, this is because your partner loves you and just wants you to be successful and happy during your retirement!

Here's the third tier. This one is really going to make you nervous. Since the IRS controls RMDs, we have zero control over how much we must withdraw in a given year. That is potentially really bad. Again, let's think this through. What happens if Uncle Sam wakes up one day and finds himself a little short on cash? I know, I know…. Uncle Sam, broke? What are the chances! Humor me anyway.

Uncle Sam could solve that problem in a handful of ways, few of which would be particularly exciting for the rest of us as tax payers. Uncle Sam could print money in order to pay the debt. This would create hyperinflation and destroy the value of our money and economy. He could raise taxes, which has been done over and over. Historically, it's the solution of choice when Uncle Sam has felt the need for more income. However, a lot of people don't vote for officials who promise to raise their taxes—especially when they feel tax rates to be onerous already. An income raise for Uncle Sam is an income loss for the average tax payer.

One way to create revenue without printing money, or *technically* raising tax rates, would be to increase the RMD amount forced upon baby boomers in retirement. After all, it is a well-established fact that most Americans' life savings are tied up in a traditional tax-deferred IRA type savings vehicle. This is money that has never been taxed. Why not increase the RMD on it? Our progressive tax system would naturally create more tax revenue as a result – even without an official marginal tax rate increase. Even better: why not do both? Raise taxes and RMD amounts! (Trust me, I didn't just give Congress an idea they hadn't already thought of.) My point is: Do you really want to be married to the IRS in retirement?

10,000 x 65 x 365 = Big Trouble

To switch metaphors, funding an IRA is like taking on a business partner. But the difference between this business partner and a normal business partner is *"YUGE,"* as they say in New York City. This business partner (the IRS) has the power to raise his percentage of ownership in the business at any time, and throw you in jail if you don't agree! Who in their right mind would go into business with a partner like that?

But it's even worse in reality.

How can it be worse?

This business partner is a hopeless spendaholic! He cannot stop himself from spending your money. To make matters worse, he's dead broke. He has to borrow money every day just to pay his current bills, let alone his mounting future bills. What are the chances a broke partner who can't stop spending money, and has the right to increase his percentage of ownership in the business, won't wake up one day and decide to solve his need for additional cash by doing exactly that—increasing his percentage of ownership in your "joint business venture"?

Oops. Another *unintended* consequence.

Yet the word *unintended* connotes innocent randomness—"just bad luck." How is it then that these "random" *unintended* consequences seem to always end up in Wall Street and Uncle Sam's favor? That's not very random, is it? At some point, the question which begs answering is, "Who really won here? Was it you and I, or was it Wall Street and Uncle Sam?"

Obviously, the 401k/IRA retirement strategy is rife with potential hazard. *Maybe* it all works out fine. *Certainly*, it isn't what most Americans have been conditioned to believe.

While one could argue the intent was to create a win-win situation, here is what we know to be true. During the era of the IRA stock market explosion, the wealth gap between the Wall Street elite and those in the underclass has grown by an exponential factor. Incomes on Wall Street have skyrocketed.

The opulent excess in lifestyle among the elite could probably feed half the world over. On the other side of the economic fence, the average underclass baby boomer worries whether he'll be able to keep his house until he dies or be forced to sell the home to pay for food, medical care, heat, and electricity. While the current system *has* worked for *some*, most in the underclass would proclaim that it has worked for far too few and failed far too many. Normal, average, everyday people can't afford to lose money, because the vast majority of those people will never truly have more money than they need.

As a generation, baby boomers enjoyed a period of unprecedented peace and prosperity and earned more money than the two generations behind them. Still, the vast majority are concerned they won't have enough money to pay for everyday living expense throughout retirement, let alone long-term health care costs. How did *that* happen? The number one concern of baby boomers in retirement is that they will outlive their money. Does that sound like a raging success?

That's failure, my friend. We must fix the failure for this and future generations!

The balance of this book will be dedicated to understanding strategies that can help circumvent the unintended consequences rampant within the current retirement system. These strategies can position those who have managed to accumulate *something* into a place that offers guarantees, peace of mind, and longevity of income during the golden years we call "retirement."

Part IV.

Understanding Safe Money Income and Retirement Strategies

Chapter Eleven.

Why a Tax-Free Retirement is More than Just a Good Idea

Why is a tax-free income strategy important for those planning retirement income today?

Hindsight is always 20/20. Back in 1980 when many Americans first began funding an IRA or 401k, the status of our nation's government was significantly different—especially as it related to our national debt and the burden of social welfare programs such as Social Security and Medicare.

Even then, watchmen stood atop the tower of financial policymaking and warned us about the perils of big government spending programs. Nevertheless, few Americans of that day could have imagined that by 2018 we would rack up over $21 trillion of national debt. In 1980, "trillion" was barely even a number. We were still trying to explain to the average person exactly how much a billion was. When our GDP (not debt) finally hit one trillion dollars in 1980, the term "trillion" was more like using the term "gazillion." For most, it was just a euphemism that meant "more money that you could possibly imagine." Today, we don't owe a single trillion. We owe $21 trillion. That's twenty-one times more money than you can imagine!

One of the factors most likely to affect the money Americans have in IRAs is *interest* on that national debt. Today, U.S. taxpayers are blessed with all-time historic low interest rates. These rates make servicing that $21 trillion debt somewhat manageable in the short term, albeit still very painful. But as interest rates begin to climb, so does the minimum service payment on that $21 trillion debt. What would happen to the average household if the interest on its mortgage payment double or tripled? Might the average household need to increase its revenues somehow? The interest on our national debt in 2016 represented about 6% of all federal spending.[31] This makes interest the fourth largest budget item.[32] Understand, that's just the interest. It doesn't touch the principal. We borrow more money every second of every day.

As concerned as every American ought to be about the mounting interest on our national debt, three other bloodsucking monsters will likely suck the life out of us long before interest on the national debt does. They are Social Security, Medicare, and Medicaid. Baby boomers will soon rely heavily upon all three of these programs. By 2016, those three programs already represent almost 50% of total federal spending.[33] Put another way, they account for almost 50 cents of every dollar our country spends within the known federal budget. That makes these three programs profoundly expensive. Just how profound of a problem could these three programs present in the future?

As of 2017, roughly two thirds of baby boomers have yet to turn 65 years of age.[34]

This means that two thirds of all baby boomers are not yet drawing upon all three programs. (Medicare is generally the last program to be drawn upon, with eligibility set at age 65.) The financial pressure of Social Security and

31 Anna Malinovskaya and Louise Sheiner, "The Hutchins Center Explains: Federal Budget Basics," May 23, 2017. Accessed May 15, 2018 at https://www.brookings.edu/blog/up-front/2016/06/01/the-hutchins-center-explains-federal-budget-basics/.

32 Kimberly Amadeo, "Interest on the National Debt and How It Affects You," March 19, 2018. Accessed May 15, 2018 at https://www.thebalance.com/interest-on-the-national-debt-4119024.

33 Anna Malinovskaya and Louise Sheiner, "The Hutchins Center Explains: Federal Budget Basics," May 23, 2017. Accessed May 15, 2018 at https://www.brookings.edu/blog/up-front/2016/06/01/the-hutchins-center-explains-federal-budget-basics/.

34 Matthew Frankel, "9 Baby-Boomer Statistics That Will Blow You Away," July 29, 2017. Accessed May 15, 2018 at https://www.fool.com/retirement/2017/07/29/9-baby-boomer-statistics-that-will-blow-you-away.aspx.

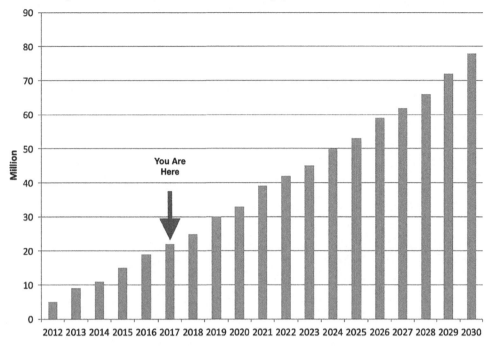

Medicare combined has the potential to virtually bankrupt the US economy as baby boomers begin to reach full participation. One could argue that never in the history of our country have we faced such a certain financial drain on our federal tax revenues. The math behind the support of these programs is filled with peril *today*, let alone in the next twenty to thirty years. Where will we get the money?

To put it all into perspective: What would happen if two thirds of all baby boomers began participating in all three programs tomorrow? The math pushes those programs to a tipping point, requiring nearly 100% of every federal dollar spent. That's at only 66.3% of baby boomers participating. At 100% participation, **far more than 100% of every dollar** would be eaten up by these three financial behemoths. We're already forced to borrow money every year to meet our current federal spending obligations.

In 2014, the Congressional Budget Office (CBO) projected the debt that the U.S. government would accumulate under current federal policies.[35] See the following chart.[36]

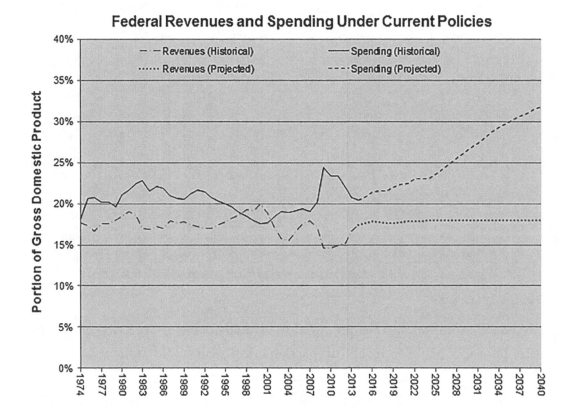

Federal Revenues and Spending Under Current Policies

Again, one might ask the reasonable question: How are we going to meet this burgeoning obligation for growth in tax revenues? If your neighbor thinks taxes are going anywhere but *up* over the long term, it's because he believes in Santa Claus and the Tooth Fairy too.

Again, one might reasonably ask: Where will we get the money?

Thankfully, we have until 2029 before we reach that 100% participation rate day. That gives us 11 years at the writing of this book to grow our economy and tax revenues sufficiently to meet burgeoning obligations in the future. To meet this future obligation, tax revenues must double over that period of time.

---

35   Report: "The 2014 Long-Term Budget Outlook." Congressional Budget Office, July 2014. Accessed May 15, 2018 at https://www.cbo.gov/publication/45471.

36   Just Facts "National Debt." Accessed May 15, 2018 at https://www.justfacts.com/nationaldebt.asp.

However, is it realistic to assume tax revenues could double in that 11-year period? Only a fool would take that bet! Even if tax revenues did double over the next 11 years, we would still be spending 50 cents of every tax dollar on these three programs—assuming no other line item in the government budget grew during that 11-year period *and interest rates remained near all-time lows*! In order to double federal tax revenues in an 11-year period, revenues would have to do something they have never done before in our nation's history: grow at an annual rate of 6.55% per year *for 11 consecutive years.*

Growing a mature first-world economy at the rate of 6.55% is nearly impossible. Even if our economy did grow that much *one year,* it would have a snowball's chance in Hades of sustaining that kind of growth for eleven consecutive years.

The best chance for sustained growth like this could only come from a demographic "people boom." Economies grow when consumption grows. Higher consumption occurs most naturally and predictable when there are more qualified consumers, also known as *people*. People are the fundamental driver of consumption, and consumption drives economic growth.

America needs more consumers. Consumers drive demand. Demand drives sales revenues. Sales revenues drives economic expansion. America desperately needs a second "population boom" to drive continued economic expansion strong enough to overcome the coming costs of an aging population positioned to become an increasing of drain on public entitlement and welfare programs such as pensions, Social Security, Medicare, and Medicaid.

Unfortunately, people booms are much harder for the financial elite on Wall Street to create by fiat declaration. The Federal Reserve Bank may be able to print money by fiat declaration. They can't print people. In the decades lurking around the corner, America will be faced with a substantial increase of people (baby boomers) slowing their *contribution* to the tax base while simultaneously increasing their *draw* against that tax base. Unless an epidemic that is only fatal to baby boomers sweeps across the nation, there is bound to be an enormous amount of "bloodletting" in our national income tax program. It is necessary if our government intends to keep even half of the promises it has made to baby boomers over the years. However, Uncle Sam won't be the one "letting" his blood. You and I will do the bloodletting. Much like the lore of vampirism, Uncle Sam will likely be the blood-sucking beneficiary—of our bloodletting.

Once again, I ask … where will we get the money? Will the world's super wealthy give up their wealth to fill the gap of national need? Or will the wealth come from the usual place—the underclass workforce trailing the baby boomers? These two generations haven't seen an average wage increase in over twenty years, and nearly a third of Millennials still live in the basement of their parents at age 30.[37] If we confiscated their entire income, it would not solve our unfunded liability problem, let alone the $21 trillion existing liability problem—also technically unfunded!

Good luck and Godspeed drawing blood from that turnip!

How about this as an *outside possibility*: Uncle Sam looks around and says, "Hey, here's where we can get the money we need. We'll raise taxes, and raise RMD amounts on baby boomers' IRAs, *and* lower the age at which one must begin taking RMDs!" (You are probably thinking by now I'd make a great Senator.)

I can almost promise you that this idea has already been discussed behind closed doors in smoke-filled congressional meeting rooms. You honestly think it hasn't?

Baby boomers would be well served to realize that there are two major risks they will need to mitigate where the future value of their 401ks and IRAs are concerned. We've talked about one of those risks extensively throughout this book: market risk. A massive prolonged crash in the debt-financed stock and bond market bubble could destroy the life savings of a substantial number of baby boomers who have failed to save a significant amount of money outside of the stock and bond markets. This represents well over ninety percent of all baby boomers' wealth for those who **have managed to save** for their retirement.

The second risk, mathematically speaking, is every bit as real as the first. That risk is the upward pressure baby boomers will soon place on the federal tax revenues needed to support the entitlements they have promised to themselves.

37 Reid Wilson, "More Millennials Living with Parents," April 24, 2017. Accessed May 15, 2018 at http://thehill.com/homenews/state-watch/330279-more-millennials-living-with-parents.

The Common English Version (CEV) of the Book of Proverbs says in Proverbs 22:3,

"When you see trouble coming, don't be stupid and walk right into it—be smart and hide."

Here's a thought. It might be wise to begin "hiding" one's money from the IRS, instead of maintaining storage of one's money in the "arrangement" created by the IRS that we talked about back in Chapter 9. Sooner or later, the tax man is bound to feel enormous pressure for increased revenue. And as that pressure mounts, rest assured he will be coming for your IRA.

The Distribution Side of an IRA

Let's consider the implications of what a tax-deferred savings plan really means as one begins retirement, the distribution phase of one's financial life.

If you've accumulated $1,000,000 in an IRA today and owe an effective tax rate of 20%, this means you really only have $800,000. Why? Because you owe $200,000 to the IRS, of course. The money you sacrificed and saved is not all yours. That's how the IRA/IRS partnership works. You have a partner in your "retirement business."

What if that scenario were to flip on its head? What if you owed an effective tax rate of 80%? That would create a tax liability of $800,000 owed to the IRS against the $1,000,000 in _your_ IRA. OUCH! Now you're left with only $200,000. How is that any different than a market loss? Either way you have A LOT LESS to live on.

"Jeff," you say, "That could never happen."

Here we go again with that word, "never"! The truth is, history would support the opposite. We've already seen top historical marginal tax rates above

90%, as illustrated in the chart below. So you really can't say it could never happen—at least not with a straight face, because it has already happened![38]

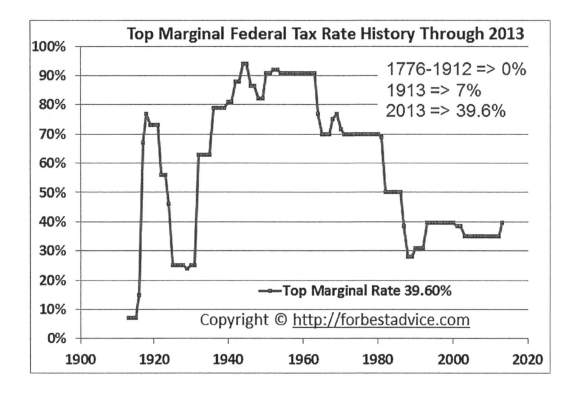

Top Marginal Federal Tax Rate History Through 2013

1776-1912 => 0%
1913 => 7%
2013 => 39.6%

—□—Top Marginal Rate 39.60%

Copyright © http://forbestadvice.com

What is it they say about history and its tendency to repeat?

Can you hear the tax man coming yet?

Even if tax rates manage to stay below 80%, many tax economists today would say that no one in their right mind should be jumping to bet against lower taxes (long-term) over the next 40 years, as baby boomers live out their retirement years. Acting now by taking steps to protect as much of the taxable income exposed in a traditional IRA would just seem a prudent endeavor to begin. An endeavor more profitably begun sooner rather than later! Why? Because the IRS wants to put time in between you and your ability to legally shelter money it feels it has a moral and legal right to confiscate!

As I present these hard mathematical facts to clients and advisers around the country, the common question that people immediately ask is:

38 ForBestAdvice, "US Top Marginal Tax Rates." Accessed May 15, 2018 at http://forbestadvice.com/Money/Taxes/Federal-Tax-Rates/Historical_Federal_Top_Marginal_Tax_Rates_History_Graph.html

"Is there a way to reduce my exposure to all of this risk and to do this legally with Safe Money Strategies?"

The answer is, yes. And it lies, in part, within the secret asset you probably don't own enough of— permanent cash value life insurance!

Chapter Twelve.

The Secret Life Insurance Asset – The LFLP

Okay. So you probably think you don't like life insurance. I get it. I hear it all the time! For years, people have been brainwashed and taught to believe that permanent cash value life insurance is a terrible investment. Well, investment strategies are often like fashion strategies. Back in the 70s when I was in junior high school, all my friends said short hair was a terrible hairstyle, and a pair of straight-legged jeans was a terrible fashion style. They were right, and it was true … until it wasn't true a few years later. Then they were wrong! Today, people who say that permanent cash value life insurance is a terrible value as a wealth building tool are wrong. Mathematically, provably, wrong! You may think you don't like life insurance—but you surely do like making money, don't you?

Solomon wrote in the Book of Wisdom known as Ecclesiastes,

"There is a time for everything, and a season **for every activity** under the heavens"

"Every activity under the heavens" would include a time for investing in permanent cash value life insurance. That "time" is particularly appealing today, as we consider our nation's fiscal plight and the danger of rising taxes. This would be especially true if cash value life insurance offered a *tax-free source of income* during the days Uncle Sam is most likely to be broke and most desperate to raise tax rates and increase tax revenues!

Guess what? It does! Cash value life insurance can offer its owner a source of non-taxable income if properly designed and executed.

Powerful Living Benefits

While the crown jewel of life insurance is always the tax-free death benefit, here's what most people don't understand about permanent cash value life insurance. Most people have been purposely (and incorrectly) taught to believe that the **only benefit** of owning a life insurance policy is the death benefit. It's the old catch-22 axiom, "Yes, but I have to die to get it!" Unless you're buying the kind of life insurance Wall Street Financial Advisers typically recommend—term life insurance—the reality is that nothing could be further from the truth. Term life insurance notwithstanding, permanent cash value life insurance policies often have tremendous *living benefits*. I like to call a policy with these living benefits an "LFLP" (Leveraged For Life Policy).

What do I mean by leveraged for life? An LFLP allows the owner to leverage multiple *cash benefits* contained within the policy—**while still living**! These living benefits are powerful financial tools. Some of the living benefits are connected to the cash value accumulation account within the policy. Other living benefits, ironically, are actually *connected* to the death benefit.

The point is this: In an LFLP, you don't have to die in order to *benefit from* (utilize) the policy's death benefit.

I can already hear the objections.

"Jeff, are you sure about that? Because I'm pretty sure my broker—who has a life insurance license—told me that the death benefit was only available to my beneficiaries after I die. How can I access the death benefit before I die? Isn't that why they call it a *death* benefit?"

Yes, it is why they call it a *death* benefit. And no, it's not *only* placed there to be used after your death—at least not in the modern *investment-grade* life insurance policy I call an LFLP.

Your broker may have a life insurance license, yes. But I promise you, it's not for the purpose of utilizing life insurance in a prolific, competent, and comprehensive manner, as a serious financial planning tool.

Look, brokers get paid to sell *"securities" products*. Do you expect a car salesman to sell fishing boats? In a broker's mind, guaranteed permanent cash value life insurance is a terrible way to prepare for your retirement future *because his brokerage firm can't make any money on it*. This product is one of his **competitors**! Of course he doesn't think you should buy it. Especially not cash value life insurance! Selling it wouldn't serve his company's interest at all! Generally, his knowledge of such products is limited to worst-case scenarios. Of course he thinks these are all bad. But that would be like saying every stock is bad because all you know about are the bad companies whose stocks have always been awful: "Yeah, my grandfather bought that stock years ago and it was awful.... So all stocks must be awful."

The car you buy today is not like the car your grandfather bought 50 years ago. Nor is today's *investment grade LFLP* like your grandfather's life insurance product of 50 years ago. Financial products should be chosen because of an individual's unique circumstance and need. Needs and climates change with time. It's all about selecting the right combination of financial tools, at the right time, in order to efficiently accomplish the client's set of financial objectives (needs).

To illustrate, let me share a story. Though based on true events, this story is fictional. The names and dollar amounts have been altered to protect privacy. Nevertheless, the story is one which I encounter on a regular basis as I meet with new clients every year.

Tom and Sue attended one of my dinner seminars earlier this month. Now they're sitting in my office discussing their financial state. I've learned that Tom and Sue are both retired, living solely on Social Security. They still owe $67,000 on their mortgage and have credit card debt of over $10,000. I ask, "How much do you have set aside in emergency cash savings?" Tom looks at me, mystified:

"What cash savings?" They have none. At this point, I began to wonder why they felt a need to meet with me. How could I possibly help these two wonderful people? They were cash broke and in debt!

I ask to see their stock portfolio. Tom pulls out the latest statement and hands it to me. The statement reveals to me that Tom and Sue have just over $70,000 in the brokerage account—every penny of which is invested in just a handful of stocks. Surprised, I look up and ask, "Is this it? Do you have anything else?" Tom says, "No."

Here are two good people in their late 60s. They have a total debt of $77,000—that's the $10,000 in credit card debt added to the $67,000 mortgage. When we factor in the $70,000 in the brokerage statement, they have a net worth of *negative $7,000.*

"How long have you had this brokerage account?" I ask. Tom replies, "We opened it within the last year."

"Well, where was your money before this?" "It was just sitting in the bank, earning zero. That's why we wanted to do something different with it—because it was earning zero."

Now I am beginning to grow a bit angry. How could anyone recommend to this couple that they take their entire liquid cash savings and place it in a position of risk? If Tom were to pass away, Sue's income from Social Security would be reduced so much that she would be unable to pay the mortgage and cover day-to-day living expenses.

I gently point this out to them. They tell me, "Before coming to your seminar, we knew nothing about money, retirement planning, or investing. Whenever we visit our current financial adviser, we just trust his recommendations, because his company is a large reputable investment company. We assume he has to know what he is doing."

Tom continues, "I worry about losing the little bit of money we have been able to save. I'm 68, not in the best health, and all I really want is to cover funeral costs and ensure Sue can stay in our home." Those are eminently reasonable priorities. Unfortunately, nothing in the investment strategy his current adviser had recommend accomplished any of Tom's goals! In fact, this advice had decreased the chance that Tom's money would do what he needed and wanted it to do. Apparently, all Tom's Wall Street adviser heard was that Tom and Sue were unhappy earning zero.

Such financial "selective hearing" is what I encounter over and over. Too many advisers seem interested only in fitting a client into a mold that serves the adviser and his firm, instead of creating a mold that fits the client and their need.

Tom and Sue have no emergency funds—not even enough to replace their refrigerator if it died one day. Not to mention the roof, air conditioner, heater, and any number of other home-related items! What if Tom or Sue have an unexpected medical bill? Worse, what if these things happen during a market downturn? Tom and Sue would take a double hit against their life savings: a *market loss* on top of *spending down* an asset unexpectedly. None of this would help Tom eliminate Sue's risk of losing everything if Tom passed away first.

Is there a better possible solution? Is there a solution built on a no-market-risk strategy?

Absolutely!

What would have happened if Tom and Sue had instead purchased two permanent LFLP life insurance policies? The policies' initial benefits would have cost about $5,000 total. The remaining $65,000 would be stored within the policies' safe liquid cash value accounts. These no-market-risk cash value accounts could have been growing at 4% (or more) instead of the zero point something Tom was getting in his bank CD account. Within three years, the one-time $5,000 policy cost could have essentially been "rebated" back to Tom and Sue's cash value accounts in the form of guaranteed interest and potential dividends. At that point, Tom and Sue could have had their original $70,000 back, stored safely in a liquid cash value account growing steadily at 4%, or more. PLUS A PERMANENT TAX-FREE DEATH BENEFIT FOR EACH OF THEM! (More details below.)

Why in the world would anyone recommend that Tom and Sue place any of this money at risk—let alone all of it? Even if their money doubled over the next 10 years, it wouldn't change their life. But if they lost even a part of it, that could hurt them severely.

Life insurance is often a much better financial tool for someone who needs to **store liquid cash savings** today. Admittedly, the numbers in the preceding example are small. But it's not about how much money people have. It's about doing what is right, sane, efficient, and best suited to a client's individual circumstances. Life insurance was the best way to leverage what little cash these two fine people had accumulated, and to maximize the most competitive interest growth potential, while protecting them from potential losses associated with risk (and fees) from which, once absorbed, they likely would never have been able to recover.

Living Larger than Life at 75

Let's look at a different fictional example that I often find mirrored in real life. This time we'll consider another *fictional someone* with a much larger amount of cash.

Mary is a 75-year-old widow. She has a stable pension income and Social Security benefits. Between the two sources of income, she is more than able to meet her current living expenses. She has no debt. Her problem (as she sees it) is the $1,000,000 of cash she has sitting in a bank CD earning just above zero point something in interest. The CD is about to come due, and she really would like to do better than what a new CD will offer, which today is another year of zero point something. However, Mary doesn't want to tie up her money for a long period of time. She has family who may need her financial help in the future. Mary has an additional $85,000 sitting in a separate bank checking account (also at zero point something). While her current income is more than sufficient to meet her living expenses, she has no plan in place to help cover future chronic illness or long-term medical care costs.

Mary has spoken with a broker who works at her bank. He recommended a conservative investment-grade bond portfolio as a solution to her desire to get a better yield on her money, rather than the bank's CD offers. But is that really the best use of Mary's cash?

I asked Mary, "Did the bank's financial planning representative present any other financial instruments or alternative strategies?" She said, "Nothing apart from another CD."

Why was the bond and CD strategy the only recommendations from the broker at her bank? Why not offer a cash value LFLP (Leveraged For Life Policy)? Truly, I don't know. I'm just speculating, but might it have been because the bank her adviser worked for doesn't make money on the sale of a life insurance policy?

Too often, this is how the game is played. To the conventional Wall Street financial adviser's advantage, Mary has been conditioned to trust her bank's adviser. Haven't we all? Surely this clean-cut, well-mannered, highly articulate gentleman with the tailored suit, who works for one of the largest banks in the world and sports a business card with a long line of capital letters following his name—surely he can be trusted to point Mary toward the product that would best meet her desire, financial need, and life situation.

And so, bonds it is. But what about bonds? Is there an argument for a better alternative?

Here's the safe money argument against a bond portfolio. First, contrary to what Wall Street tries to lead us to believe, a bond portfolio is not safe from market risk. The only thing an investment grade bond portfolio buys Mary is the promise of a fixed-income yield averaging today somewhere in the 3%–3.5% range. But to regain liquidity (access) to her cash if she needed it, Mary would have to sell the bond—which exposes her principal to the potential of loss, i.e. market risk! If Mary decided to sell the bond, although it may not feel like it, at that point her money would be in a position of 100% risk. Bond prices go up and down every day with changes in the interest rate markets. In addition, even large, long stable companies file bankruptcy and go out of business. (Remember GM, Enron, Globecomm, Bear Stearns, Lehman Brothers, etc., just to name a recent few!)

Mary likely has more cash than she will ever need. She just needs a safe and liquid place to store it, preferably one offering a moderate return rate. Mary wants to maintain her wealth, while having the necessary cash liquidity to assist her family, maintain her home, maintain her automobile, and cover unexpected out-of-pocket healthcare costs. This cash liquidity will allow Mary to continue living independently.

I'll ask the question again. Why not an LFLP life insurance plan?

"But Jeff, Mary is 75 years old."

Yes, but that doesn't mean Mary can't buy life insurance.

"But won't it cost her a small fortune?"

Fortunes, like all other things, are relative. Why not let Mary make the decision after she knows the facts?

Here are the facts.

Because Mary is still in relatively good health at age 75, she qualifies for a permanent whole life cash-value life insurance product called a *Single Premium Life Insurance policy*. Remember the LFLP? If Mary were to purchase such a policy, here's how the math works within the policy provisions.

Mary would purchase the policy for $1,000,000 in a single premium, a one-time payment. (Remember Mary still has $85,000 in another account for emergencies, not to mention her regular income.) The single premium of one million dollars could immediately secure a guaranteed tax-free death benefit of $1,395,000. (All numbers from this point on are based on Mary's health assumptions and underwriting guidelines of a triple-A rated life insurance company.) Mary's policy would also generate an immediate liquid cash value account of $896,000. At the end of year one, by reinvesting her interest and non-guaranteed year-end dividends back into the policy, Mary's total cash value would be $913,500, with a death benefit of $1,412,000.

From that point on, if Mary continues reinvesting the interest and earned dividends, her cash value could grow at approximately 4%, or more each year. 4% is much higher than zero!

By year four, Mary could have recovered the cost of insurance on her initial premium. The liquid cash value account could have been sitting at $1,040,182 and still growing. Mary would have 100% liquidity to her cash—she could access it anytime without penalty or fear of market risk. Mary would also have purchased a permanent tax-free death benefit of $1,412,000.

Did you hear that? Mary could have compounding cash growth at 4% or more, 100% liquidity, and a $1.4 million tax-free death benefit—all with *zero* market risk to her principal! How much market risk does a bond portfolio have? 100%, that's how much! In addition, because this is a LFLP policy, beginning in year one, Mary can also have access to $1,095,822 tax free if she develops a chronic illness under the policy's provisions, and a $1,109,626 tax free terminal illness care benefit.

Compare the Math!

Let's review.

- Bonds: 100% market risk and a potential 3.0% to 4.0% interest yield.

- LFLP: 0% market risk and potential 4% to 5% yield.[39]

Now to be sure, Mary would have to incur a net cost of $86,500 in year one to purchase the policy. (When we offset the $1,000,000 premium with the $913,500 cash value, the net cost is $86,500.) But here's what that money bought Mary:

1. A permanent tax-free death benefit asset worth 16 times its cost of $86,500.

2. A cash value savings account growing tax-deferred with zero market risk.

3. The potential of a *growing* tax-free death benefit asset as Mary continues to live.

4. An immediate tax-free living benefit for Chronic Illness Care worth $95,822 more than the one-time premium Mary paid.

5. A tax-free living benefit for Terminal Illness Care worth $109,626 more than the one-time premium Mary paid.

---

39 Growth assumptions are based upon the offers of multiple "A" rated life insurance carriers at the time of writing. Guarantees and declared dividend rates are subject to change at any time in the future.

Let's consider items number 4 and 5 more closely.

Mary could have a tax-free living benefit for Chronic Illness Care of $1,095,822. That's $95,822 **more** than her total premium of $1,000,000. She also could have a tax-free Terminal Illness Living Benefit of $1,195,626. That's $195,626 more than her total premium. *Both benefits* have the potential to grow each year as non-guaranteed dividends are paid and reinvested into the policy. Many high-quality life insurance companies today are over a century old and have never missed paying a single year of dividends in their history.

Remember, at age 75, Mary has no long-term care or terminal care policy in place. If she becomes sick and needs chronic care, then she can get a statement from her doctor saying she needs assistance in any two of the six ADLs (Activities of Daily Living). That statement would trigger a provision in the LFLP insurance policy that provides an extra $95,822. If Mary lives to be 85 and then needs chronic illness care, her tax-free *living benefit* could have grown to $1,440,314. Mary could have 44% more than her initial first-year premium of $1,000,000, without it costing her a single additional penny out of pocket, and without risking a single penny of her wealth. Her total cash value at age 85 could have grown as high as $1,309,540, with a death benefit as high as $1,697,068. All of this liquidity, growth, and leverage could be accomplished without assuming a single penny of market risk.

Mary doesn't know what the future holds. Will she fall and break a hip bone and need assisted chronic living care in the future? Will she live out her years with the relative good health she enjoys now and pass away in her sleep? Will she or a family member enter an unforeseen challenging financial period in which an unexpected need for cash or increased income arises?

What the future holds is anyone's guess. What is certain is that by executing this financial strategy and obtaining the leverage of an LFLP, Mary has created the ability to "roll with the punches," whatever life throws at her. She has preserved her liquidity and access to cash. She has placed the cash in a vehicle that offers a reasonable growth rate with no market risk. And if Mary needs long term chronic illness care, she has a substantial "extra" sum of **tax free cash** to draw upon. (As opposed to the Wall Street bond portfolio strategy her banker recommended, from which she would have had to pay taxes—*if* she could have liquidated the bond at a profit.) And, when Mary passes away, she will have left behind a meaningful, immediate, guaranteed, **tax-free** death benefit for her beneficiaries.

With an LFLP, Mary is able to leverage each individual dollar in four different directions. Mary doesn't know what the future holds. But she knows this financial instrument is engineered with the flexibility to leverage multiple built-in contingencies that can help her address many of life's lingering financial obstacles—even while she is alive! That's the beauty of an LFLP financial planning strategy.

But Mary was never shown this remarkable option ... until she met with a qualified life insurance and retirement income planner.

Chapter Thirteen.

College Planning and Tax-Free Retirement with an LFLP

Let's look at another powerful example of how permanent cash value life insurance in an LFLP could prove to be a tremendous asset when leveraged for college planning (along with a possible tax-free income in retirement).

Jim and Anne are a married couple, both 40 years of age. Anne is a stay-at-home mom raising three children, now 9, 6, and 4 years old. Jim has a 401k totaling $202,500. Jim's annual income is $135,000. His employer matches his 401k contributions up to 3% of his salary, which equals $4,050 per year. Jim and Anne have budgeted to save $10,000 per year for retirement. Jim has a life insurance policy through his employer with a death benefit of five times his base salary: $675,000. Since his mortgage has only $182,000 left to pay, he feels as though the $675,000 life policy through his employer is a sufficient amount of life insurance. Jim and Anne's financial planner suggested an equities-based 529 college plan for each of their four children, which they began funding at $10,000 per year just this past year.

Once again, permanent cash value life insurance is nowhere to be found. Every penny of invested savings has been earmarked for a product that includes 100% risk of principal. In truth, Jim has a plan for college **IF-come** in the future. The problem with the plan for Jim is there is no **IF** in his family's future needs. His kids *will* need money for college. He and Anne *will* need income down the road during retirement. Might Jim be well served to have a secondary plan for **IN-*come*** instead of **IF-*come*** to help meet these ***certain*** financial needs he and his family **will have** in the future?

What if the market crashed and 30%–70% of the 529 college savings plan were lost just as Jim and Anne's firstborn graduates high school?

Solving the FAFSA Problem

More mundanely, every penny in a traditional tax deferred plan will count against Jim's FAFSA numbers and hurt his ability to qualify for financial aid, such as government grant programs, loans, and college-based aid programs. But money accumulated in a cash value life insurance policy does not count as an asset against FAFSA filings. To the IRS, for FAFSA purposes, cash value in a life insurance policy is completely invisible! This unique strategic benefit can be the key to obtaining thousands of extra dollars for college aid.

Guaranteed cash. Guaranteed growth. Plus FAFSA benefits! Oh yes, and a guaranteed death benefit to ensure Anne and the children are always taken care of should Jim be taken from his family as the primary breadwinner prematurely.

To help illustrate the enormous risk of failure Jim is assuming in the traditional savings strategy recommended by his traditional Wall Street broker, let's assume Jim turned 40 in December of 1999 and began funding his children's 529 on December 31, 1999. He continues funding for the next 9 years until his oldest son is ready to enter his freshman year in college. The account performance equals the S&P 500 index returns with dividends reinvested each year. See chart on next page.

Jim begins the calendar in January 2000 with a pre-tax deposit of $10,000 already in his account from his deposit on December 31, 1999. He then continues making deposits on December 31 of each year through the end of 2008.

That makes a total of 9 deposits of $10,000 each, a cumulative $90,000 in contributions.

S&P 500 Index with Dividends Reinvested*

*Source: https://ycharts.com/indicators/sandp_500_total_return_annual

Month	Year	Client Age	Beginning Account Value	One Year Index Return	Management Fee	Change In Value	Year End Contribution	Year End Value
Jan - Dec	(1) 2000	40	$ 10,000	-9.10%	-1.50%	$ 8,940	$ 10,000	$ 18,940
Jan - Dec	(2) 2001	41	$ 18,940	-11.89%	-1.50%	$ 16,404	$ 10,000	$ 26,404
Jan - Dec	(3) 2002	42	$ 26,404	-22.10%	-1.50%	$ 20,173	$ 10,000	$ 30,173
Jan - Dec	(4) 2003	43	$ 30,173	28.68%	-1.50%	$ 38,374	$ 10,000	$ 48,374
Jan - Dec	(5) 2004	44	$ 48,374	10.88%	-1.50%	$ 52,911	$ 10,000	$ 62,911
Jan - Dec	(6) 2005	45	$ 62,911	4.91%	-1.50%	$ 65,056	$ 10,000	$ 75,056
Jan - Dec	(7) 2006	46	$ 75,056	15.79%	-1.50%	$ 85,782	$ 10,000	$ 95,782
Jan - Dec	(8) 2007	47	$ 95,782	5.49%	-1.50%	$ 99,603	$ 10,000	$109,603
Jan - Dec	(9) 2008	48	$ 109,603	-37.00%	-1.50%	$ 67,406	$ 10,000	$ 77,406
			Gross Total Return	-14.34%				
		Average Annual Return After Fees		**-3.09%**				

As long as withdrawals in the future are used for college by Jim and Anne's children, the entire amount can be withdrawn and utilized tax-free. However, if withdraws are not used for college, they are not available as tax-free withdrawals.

In this historical example, had Jim and Anne's 529 plan matched the performance of the S&P 500 with dividends reinvested, the account would have ended up with $77,406. This is **$12,594 less than their total contributions!** Jim would have earned more by burying his money in the back yard! Too bad for Jim, Anne, and their oldest child.

And yet Jim and Anne's broker made a positive return from this risk-based strategy. Risk for Jim and Anne meant no risk and guaranteed income for Wall Street! To be fair, Jim and Anne did have the *opportunity* to make unlimited investment returns. However, in this example, they paid dearly for that privilege!

How would an LFLP have performed differently? We'll consider a conservative whole life policy, with interested and dividends reinvested at the current declaration rates available as of December 2017. In the same ten-year period here is what Jim and Anne would have had available to leverage by the time of their oldest child's freshman year in college. See below:

Year	Age	Premium	IncreaseInCashValue	CashValue	DeathBenefit
1	41	$8,500	$6,270	$6,270	$273,757
2	42	$8,500	$7,911	$14,181	$297,409
3	43	$8,500	$8,244	$22,425	$320,688
4	44	$8,500	$8,630	$31,054	$343,475
5	45	$8,500	$9,064	$40,118	$365,940
6	46	$8,500	$9,482	$49,600	$388,168
7	47	$8,500	$9,919	$59,519	$410,099
8	48	$8,500	$10,424	$69,943	$431,793
9	49	$8,500	$10,953	$80,895	$453,341

Since Jim funds the policy with post-tax instead of pre-tax dollars, he has $8,500 to contribute each year instead of $10,000. (The example assumes an effective net 15% federal tax rate.) So the premium deposits are $1,500 smaller. Thus, over the 10 years, Jim and Anne contribute $76,500 instead of $90,000. Nevertheless, Jim and Anne's college savings still has positive growth and grows to $80,895. This cash value account can be accessed **tax-free** when their first child becomes a college freshman.

Unlike the Wall Street 529 plan, the LFLP cash value account will continue to grow each subsequent year as their younger children turn 18 and begin college. Even while they are using it. More on this in a minute.

Notice something else very interesting. In year 9, Jim deposited $8,500 into his policy. But his cash value account grew **$10,953**. That's a staggering 22.3% more than he deposited!

Remember also: money accumulated in a cash value life insurance policy does not count as an asset against Jim and Anne's FAFSA filings. Cash value in a life insurance policy is completely invisible to the IRS and FAFSA! Again, this unique benefit often makes a family eligible for thousands of additional "need-based" funds in financial aid. Because of their lower FAFSA asset value, the family may also qualify for lower preferred interest rates on certain financial aid products and housing assistance. The list of benefits for maintaining low asset value where FAFSA are concerned go on and on! Each of these benefits adds to the "net return" of the LFLP college planning strategy.

The compound growth of Jim's cash value account continues over the next 11 years. See below:

10	50	$8,500	$11,507	$92,402	$474,737
11	51	$8,500	$12,101	$104,503	$495,972
12	52	$8,500	$12,615	$117,117	$516,970
13	53	$8,500	$13,138	$130,255	$537,692
14	54	$8,500	$13,688	$143,943	$558,186
15	55	$8,500	$14,244	$158,187	$578,512
16	56	$8,500	$14,826	$173,013	$598,725
17	57	$8,500	$15,423	$188,436	$618,858
18	58	$8,500	$16,053	$204,489	$638,920
19	59	$8,500	$16,704	$221,194	$658,903
20	60	$8,500	$17,377	$238,570	$678,824

In year 11, Jim deposits the same $8,500 into his account. But the account grows **$12,101**, almost 30% growth over and beyond his deposit! Understand that this will happen *even if Jim withdraws funds as a policy loan to fund a child's college.*

In year 20, Jim has contributed the same $8,500 annual deposit, yet his cash value account grew by $17,377. That's 51% more than his deposit. All of this is happening safely, **right when Jim and Anne (and their kids) need it the most!** They have zero market risk. This plan will not explode and wreck their children's college future right when they need the money the most.

Is it a fair critique to say I cherry-picked a historical time period not favorable to Wall Street? Perhaps. However, this critique by Wall Street simply misdirects us from the broader point: *uncertainty.* The question is, when planning for something as important *and certain* as our children's education, does it make sense to save money in a place of high risk and **no certainty of success**? Does it really make sense to gamble with our child's future college savings in an account that is full of risk, and thus completely unpredictable?

No! Especially when a safe, guaranteed alternative strategy exists which offers a tax-free funding source that grows cash value accounts by as much as 30%–51% more than the actual amount deposited *in the very years the kids actually* **need** *the money.*

However, it gets even better! Jim and Anne get another benefit from utilizing an LFLP whole life cash-value strategy. It's a benefit that is also absent from the traditional Wall Street 529 plan.

Let's say Jim and Anne stick with the 529 plan. What if Jim were to die before getting his kids through college? Would Anne, a stay-at-home mom, have sufficient funds to cover all her family's living expenses *and send 3 kids through college?* Well, Jim did have a tax-free death benefit of $670,000 through his employer. That sum might cover living expenses *or* send three kids through college—probably not both, especially as costs continue to rise.

Maybe Anne could get a job? Even with a college degree, Anne is unlikely to get a job where she could immediately earn as much as Jim did. Perhaps it's *possible*. But who would want to bet *their children's future* on those odds?

Maybe Anne's best option is to quickly fall in love again and marry a "Prince Charming" who is willing to assume her financial burden. But any new relationship would occur during a time of enormous grief and emotional suffering, not to mention tremendous financial pressure. Is this the sort of situation Jim would want Anne to be forced to consider? Probably not!

Might there be a better way?

Say Jim and Anne opt for the LFLP strategy instead. If Jim died 5 years into funding the LFLP, the death benefit would be $365,940. If he died 15 years into funding it, the death benefit would be $578,512. Either one of those additional amounts, on top of his $675,000 employer death benefit, would provide Anne with the funds to continue as a stay-at-home mom and complete the plan she and Jim had originally made for their children. Anne would feel far less financial pressure to launch a career late in life or remarry amid the grief of loss and emotional turmoil it is sure to bring.

But we're not finished yet. There is **still another benefit** contained within the LFLP for Jim and Anne!

Assuming Jim *does not die* prematurely, once the kids are grown and out of college, Jim and Anne's living expenses will likely drop significantly. Empty nesters are usually able to save the most money for their future during this period of time in life. Having chosen to fund a whole life cash value policy instead of a 529 plan, Jim and Anne can now use their extra income to quickly pay themselves back for the policy loans taken during their kids' college years.

You might have a question at this point, and it's a fair one. "Why is having the ability to pay a self-taken loan such a great thing? If Jim and Anne had simply depleted the savings in a traditional 529 plan, there wouldn't have been a debt to repay!" Well, yes … but not entirely.

Depleting the 529 plan to pay for college creates what is called a **lost opportunity cost**, because Jim and Anne forfeit any future compound interest on the amount they withdrew. Once the money is withdrawn, it no longer works for them by earning interest. Compounding interest on that money is gone (lost) forever.

Here's why having a loan to repay to yourself can be good. With the right life insurance company, the cash value in the LFLP policy **continues to grow** and compound annually, **even while a loan is out against it**. This is called a *participating* LFLP policy feature. It means that Jim and Anne can take a loan, pay for college, and then replenish the policy later—**while still earning compound interest on the *full cash value amount during the entire time the money is being used for college*.** No lost opportunity cost!

Because they do not lose any principal, Jim and Anne will continue to receive compound interest. **Instead of starting over with zero in year 21, because the funding source has been depleted, Jim and Anne still have $238,570 in that account available to earn compound interest!** At a modest 4% growth, that money will yield $9,542 interest the very next year—the very year they would have had to start over with zero had they funded and depleted a 529 plan. Jim and Anne do not have to deplete their life insurance policy—they simply take a *loan* out against it. The money is still there earning interest. Later, they pay the loan back "to themselves."

With the LFLP strategy, Jim and Anne can safely and comfortable guarantee themselves a substantial tax-free bucket **with no IRA rules to follow regarding when, or even how much, they are allowed to take out each year in the future**. Those funds will be available at any time, and at almost any amount they desire, large or small—all potentially tax free!

Assuming a combined federal, state, and local tax rate of 30% in later empty nester years, Jim and Anne would have had to accumulate the equivalent of **$830,387 _taxable dollars_** during those 15 empty nester years (surviving market risk) just to break even with the LFLP strategy. That's an average of an extra $55,359 per year, _again assuming_ the market has no down years during that 15-year period. Really? How likely is that? Whatever odds one places upon it, here's one thing I know for sure. The odds of it happening with the LFLP strategy are 100% better. And it would only take a loan payment of $24,156 each year—less than half of the $55,359 per year needed with the Wall Street plan! Which odds would you prefer? Which payment would you prefer? If Jim and Anne ended up being able to afford to make the total payment of $55,339 during those years, great! That just means they have an _extra $31,183 to sock away and put to work for their future and receive compound interest on for the next 15 years!_

Seriously, if you knew the facts as you know them now, which plan would you have chosen?

The choice is rather obvious. But Jim and Anne's Wall Street adviser never had this conversation with them. The option was not even on the table for Jim and Anne's consideration.

Perhaps now you're beginning to see the big picture of what Wall Street doesn't want you to know, and certainly doesn't want you to understand. This is why a safe money financial adviser is almost always disparaged by a Wall Street fee-based, risk-saturated financial planner. His positive assumption, risk-based illustrations can look beautiful on paper. But paper theories in the world of Wall Street are just that: theories. Except where a Wall Street fee on the money at risk is concerned. Those fees are real 100% of the time!

But we're not done yet. There is one more advantage to the LFLP College savings plan—and it's "YUGE"!

If Jim and Anne take out an LFLP policy plan on Jim, Anne will be protected in case Jim passes away. His guaranteed death benefit of $736,230 will be available for her. Further, Jim could have a living Chronic Illness Benefit of $593,203 and a living Terminal Illness Benefit of $637,981—both tax free! Realize that none of these "extra" benefits would be available in a Wall Street

529 college savings plan or an IRA. And in an LFLP strategy, unlike a Wall Street plan, all of this is accomplished without any market risk whatsoever! Jim and Anne are able to achieve all of this with cash value growth around 4%, possibly more. What if they were able to qualify for an LFLP that yielded 5% cash value growth? Account values that never go down and never stop growing are very hard to beat!

Now that you know and understand some of the enormous benefits an LFLP life insurance plan offers for long-term college funding or retirement savings, let's look at the need virtually all of us will face in retirement: the need for a lifetime income. Income that never ends. Income that is guaranteed to last as long as we last! Income for life.

Chapter Fourteen.

Why Guaranteed Lifetime Income Should Be a Part of Every Retiree's Financial Plan

When Social Security law was first enacted, the average life expectancy was about 62 years of age. In its beginning, an individual couldn't collect Social Security until 65 years of age. Consequently, one could say Social Security was essentially enacted to serve as an insurance policy against a person living too long. The truth was, in the early days of Social Security, the average person would never live long enough to collect it. If people did live long enough to collect it, they generally died shortly thereafter.

Not so today!

The Social Security Problem

Today the average person retiring at the age of 65 could easily live an additional 30 years in retirement. Social Security was never designed to accommodate this financial need. Moreover, when one considers the speed at which medical science is advancing today, who knows what cures will extend life expectancies further during the next 30 years? Social Security meets its promises to American workers solely by tax revenues collected from the income of Americans who are still at work. Further exasperating the problem of the math behind Social Security is the fact that as baby boomers retire, the ratio of workers supporting payments to people on Social Security has dropped. It has dropped from a high of 42:1 in 1935 (when it was first enacted) to *less* than 3:1 by the year 2010.

How Many Workers Support One Social Security Retiree?

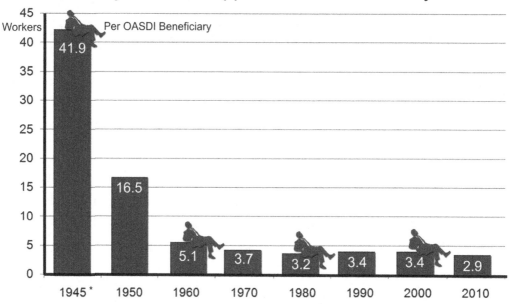

Source: 2012 OASDI Trustee Report, Table IV.B2., www.ssa.gov, accesssed May 21, 2012.
Data note: The Trustee Report provides data from 1945 and onward. Prior estimates are unavailable.
Produced by Veronique de Rugy Mercatus Center at George Mason University.

As bad as the math behind Social Security is today, this critical support ratio is projected to continue to deteriorate. According to the Social Security Administration government website:

> "Due to demographic changes, the U.S. Social Security system will face financial challenges in the near future. Declining fertility rates and increasing life expectancies are causing the U.S. population to age…. Consequently, the Social Security system is experiencing a declining worker-to-beneficiary ratio, which **will fall from 3.3 in 2005 to 2.1 in 2040….** This presents a significant challenge to policymakers."[40]

Let me translate what the government itself is saying about the staple source of most Americans' income in retirement: The math will not support the promise. There is simply not going to be enough water in the well. In fact, according to the Social Security Administration website, the well will run dry in 2040, long before many baby boomers have lived out their normal lifespan.[41]

This reality has enormous implications for those approaching retirement or currently in retirement. It is especially frightening to those who plan to lean heavily on a monthly Social Security check in order to support a portion of their basic monthly living needs or "lifestyle dream."

The Social Security website continues discussing the future sustainability of Social Security as we know. Then it makes an even more telling statement, one which perhaps prophetically telegraphs where this train is ultimately headed:

"One policy option that could help keep the Social Security system solvent is to **reduce retirement benefits,** either by raising the normal retirement age or through life expectancy indexing, to reflect the fact that people are living longer… Still **other options** would seek to **raise additional revenue** for the system."[42]

Again, allow me to translate: You will not get what you're being promised today!

---

40   Gayle L. Reznik, Dave Shoffner, and David A. Weaver, "Coping with the Demographic Challenge: Fewer Children and Living Longer," 2005/2006. Accessed January 28, 2018 at https://www.ssa.gov/policy/docs/ssb/v66n4/v66n4p37.html.

41 Ibid.

42 Ibid.

If you're planning for a certain level of income in retirement, you had better use a source other than Social Security. Whatever you thought Social Security had promised you, it's not going to happen that way.

Those entering retirement today have a profound need for a sure source of supplemental lifetime income **in addition to Social Security**. The problem is further exasperated by the death of the corporate pension. The vast majority of American workers retiring in this century will not have the benefit of a company pension to supplement guaranteed income for the next 20–30 years once in retirement. What American workers **will have** (if anything) is what they have accumulated in their tax-qualified savings plans—their 401k, 403b, SEP, SIMPLE, IRA, etc. For most, those funds are invested in account strategies that can (and do) vary in value every day. Yet Wall Street seems perfectly fine advising (convincing) Americans that there is no need for any of us to be concerned about our ability to draw certain income from those accounts in the future. Wall Street "gods" have our back!

The Wall Street Problem

Historically, the market experiences a major bear market correction of 20% or more once every 42 months on average. That amounts to once every 3.5 years.[43] That means we should expect 8.5 major market corrections during a 30-year period. During the **distribution phase** of your retirement savings, *any one of those 8.5 corrections* could potentially lead to a **total depletion** of your life savings long before you have lived out your years on planet Earth. Many savers will recall that it's hard enough to recover from a market correction and get back to "even par" *while one is still working*. While people are working, they are contributing to their accounts, and perhaps even benefiting from an employer's matching contribution. But in retirement, people are not contributing to their retirement accounts. Recovery is virtually impossible. Trying to regain lost

---

43   Jim Freeman, "Frequency of Market Corrections – Test Your Knowledge," June 8, 2012. Accessed May 15, 2018 at https://financialalternatives.com/2012/frequency-of-market-corrections-test-your-knowledge/.

money from market "corrections" could eat up your most productive, healthy, and meaningful years of retirement.

Do you remember the story of Gordon and Diane in chapter two? Gordon began his retirement with an account value of one million dollars. Gordon and his wife Diane needed a $50,000 income from the one-million-dollar account, which is a beginning drawn down of 5%. At a 5% draw down, their one-million-dollar account value would last 20 years—even if they had buried their money in the back yard! While 20 years might be long enough to carry Gordon to his life expectancy (age 85), what if Gordon *or his wife* lived to be 95? Might Gordon and Diane want a plan that ensures they not run out of income before *both of them* run out of life?

Say the market crashes 50% the year after Gordon retires. Now his one-million-dollar account is worth only $500,000. Yet Gordon and Diane still need an income of $50,000. Now their risk of running out of money just became gigantic! They are forced to withdrawal 10% of their account value to get the same $50,000 income.

How long will Gordon's life savings last if he has to take withdrawals of 10% (or more) each year? What if the market goes down another 10% the following year before it finally hits bottom?

After three years of market downturns, fees, and income withdrawals of $50,000 (plus inflation), Gordon is left with less than $300,000. Literally three years into Gordon's retirement, his account has been depleted by over 70%. The income draw he and Diane will need each year moving forward in time is now more than 17.6% of the total value of the asset. Do you see how quickly market risk can multiply and destroy Gordon and Diane's chance of success in the future?

Guaranteeing a consistent, growing lifetime income from a risk-based and Wall-Street-backed investment account borders on the absurd! You might as well be banking on the ability to pick a winning lottery ticket. If you live (gamble) long enough, the house will surely clean out your account!

Never has there been a more pressing need for retirement income strategies that protect against risk and provide for longevity of life! The truth is, Wall Street risk-based retirement strategies have no answer other than to diversify risk. The problem with the diversification *of risk*, is that **it is still *risk*!** The only difference is that when the crash of a market comes (and it will come), you'll be losing money in fifty different places, instead of only five! That's Wall Street diversification.

You don't think so?

Isn't that what happened in 2008 to millions of people? It absolutely and undeniably is! Yet these people had Wall Street financial advisers who assured them before 2008 that their investments were fully diversified.

Diversification of risk didn't save the average investor's account from dropping by 15%–25%.[44]

Honestly, how long can a person in retirement continue to afford taking their full budgeted income withdrawals after losing 50% or more in a single year? It takes a gain of 100% to replenish a loss of 50%. How long does it generally take the market to yield a 100% recovery gain—especially net of annual management broker fees?

After the dot-com bubble of 2000, it took more than seven years for the market to make it back to where it was before the crash (not net of potential management fees). How many people would advise someone they actually cared for to **risk** giving up the best, healthiest and most vibrant years of their retirement by forgoing full income withdrawals, waiting for the market to recover, and hoping they can resume regular withdrawals soon? I doubt any reading this book would make such a recommendation. Yet many financial advisers trained and conditioned by Wall Street don't hesitate to advise their clients to do exactly that. Shouldn't that bother us?

In Gordon's case, he would have been 72 before his account was made whole … only to have lightning strike a second time in 2008 and knock him completely out of the saddle again! If he and Diane waited after 2008, Gordon would have been 78 years old before his account had recovered. Do you think Gordon and Diane would still have the same energy, health, and vitality left at age 78 to do all the things they wanted to do at age 66?

---

44 Emily Brandon and Katy Marquardt, "How Did Your 401(k) Really Stack Up in 2008?," February 12, 2009. Accessed May 15, 2018 at https://money.usnews.com/money/retirement/articles/2009/02/12/how-did-your-401k-really-stack-up-in-2008?page=2.

What most retirees need today is not more of Wall Street's version of diversification—diversification **OF market risk**. What people retiring today need more of is a healthy dose of diversification **FROM market risk—and guaranteed income!**

This is the only kind of diversification that preserves one's principal during periods of systemic market downturn. Downturns are far more regular than a Wall Street Financial Planner want us to remember. Investors endured negative market downturns in years such as 1966, 1969, 1973, 1974, 1977, 1981, 1987, 1994, 2000, 2001, 2002, 2008, 2015....[45]

Preserving principal is necessary to guarantee that your savings and interest will be there when you need them as the basis for a lifetime income. When the day comes for my wife and me to begin living off of income from the assets we have spent a lifetime sacrificing to accumulate, by golly, I want those assets to be there! Not 50% of the time, not 75% of the time, not 90% of the time. They need to be there 100% of the time. Isn't that how you feel?

There are no "do overs." We all get one chance at retirement! Uncle Sam has already warned us we can't count on Social Security, at least not as we have been promised. Is not now the time to secure a lifetime income guarantee from a *stable financial institution*—one that has not broken a single financial promise in more than a century of world wars, famines, inflation, deflation, and global financial market ups and downs?

Use your retirement savings to secure a lifetime retirement income. Life insurance companies have a 400-year history of making good on their financial promises. What sort of promises? Promises today that no matter how long you live, both you and your spouse will always receive a monthly income. In the old days people called that a **pension**. Today, everyone wishes for a pension, but few actually have one. Who among us doesn't long for the good ol' days? A highly rated life insurance company is the only financial institution that can ensure you and your spouse live out your retirement—just like the good ol' days!

45 Robert Allan Schwartz, "Annual Returns Of The S&P 500 From 1928 To 2015," February 24, 2016. Accessed May 15, 2018 at https://seekingalpha.com/instablog/605212-robert-allan-schwartz/4831186-annual-returns-s-and-p-500-1928-2015.

The Wealth Problem

Wall Street would like to tempt those more fortunate among us to believe we can rely on the **abundance** of our accumulated wealth. However, the problem with wealth is that it not only can be *acquired* but also can be *lost*. Consequently, the accumulation of wealth does not in and of itself guarantee a lifetime income. The two are not the same. Poll the average American:

- Do you want a pile of wealth that you could lose?

- Or do you want permanent income you can never lose?

How many do you think would risk their future with something that could be lost, when a *guarantee of winning income* was theirs for the taking? Not many! Yet that's exactly what Wall Street wants you to choose for yourself and your spouse in retirement.

Think of it this way. Your favorite football team is about to win the Super Bowl. You are ahead by 3 points with only a minute and thirty seconds left to play in the game. Your opponent has just turned the ball over on downs and is out of time outs. All you have to do is snap the ball, have your quarterback drop to his knee, twice, and run the clock out. It's over. You've won!

What idiot coach would call a play that has the quarterback drop back, attempt to catch the opposing team off guard, and throw a pass downfield? In a best-case scenario, your team wins by 10 points instead of 3. Big deal. Calling a risky play to *maybe* win by 10 also introduces the risk of **losing** the game by fumbling the ball, or throwing an interception. The risk is not worth the reward. Absent a turnover, you are guaranteed to win the game! So what if the stats say you lost three yards by taking a knee on the final two plays of the game? Who cares? You won the championship!

Wall Street wants you to risk the championship in order to maybe win by 10 points instead of 3. Wall Street says you should risk defeat over the certain victory you have worked a lifetime to earn. It's no skin off of Wall Street's back if the risk doesn't play out in your favor and you throw an interception that gets run back for a touchdown! Heck, Wall Street still made a fee on the pass, the interception, and the opposing team's touchdown! Advisers get paid regardless of who wins, whether you, or the opponent who stands in your way—Risk!

Wall Street wants all of us to play the game of risk, from cradle to grave.

Personally, I find it ironic that people who wish they had a pension never consider "pensionizing" a portion of their accumulated wealth to ensure a lifetime income (think pension) for themselves and their spouses. It's beyond me why anyone would try to convince those of us with finite financial resources to accept a strategy promising "forever risk" instead of "forever income." Success throughout our retirement years will ultimately be defined by income—income that lasts as long as life and breath!

How do you turn your accumulated wealth into a personal pension? How do you guarantee a lifetime income with your current cash assets?

With a guaranteed fixed-income and/or fixed index annuity. Let's finish in our final chapter with the most popular retirement instrument among conservative investors today: The Fixed Index Annuity.

Chapter Fifteen.

Guaranteed Income Annuities: Features, Benefits, and Fees

A lot has been written about annuities over the last decade. As baby boomers began entering retirement years, the internet exploded with "objective" opinions from would-be financial planning experts. These internet sensations relied on blogs, YouTube, and an array of ad campaigns seen on social media sites, all pontificating about their "objective" analysis of the value of various retirement income and investment strategies.

In truth, there is no "objective" analysis. Of this you can be certain: Whatever an adviser is incentivized to sell—that is, how he makes *his* money—is what he will "objectively" recommend.

This would include myself.

The difference between me (along with any adviser who may have recommended this book) and the "other guy" is that I/we will disclose this truth to you clearly from the very beginning. Recall my opening disclosure?

I am not, do not, and will not *ever* offer advice on any securities product in this book. Period. Nothing in this book should be construed as said advice. I have no license to practice, nor offer advice, nor otherwise recommend in any way, shape, or form, to any person whatsoever, how, why, or when to buy or sell *any* securities-related product, instrument, or securities-related investment strategy.

Moreover, you would be a fool for taking such advice even if I did! I have no idea what the financial markets (or the people who may manipulate them) are going to do at any given point in time. Period.

The reader should also be aware that I do recommend, represent, and am licensed to advise and sell financial products and strategies commonly referred to as guaranteed safe money insurance contracts (a variety of annuities and various life insurance policies), which are backed solely by the claims paying ability of the life insurance companies.

While at one time, I possessed a securities license to sell risk, today I have chosen to devote my entire financial practice as a Safe Money Financial Adviser. As a Safe Money Financial Adviser, I am a big fan of guaranteed fixed-income products. I only work with products and strategies that guarantee my client's principal against market loss, and my client's income against longevity of life. I believe *protecting principal* and *providing income* are the two most important objectives for anyone approaching retirement. I know of only two financial products offering legal guarantees to accomplish these two lofty goals: Fixed Annuities (FAs) and Fixed Index Annuities (FIAs). Between the two, today, I believe the FIA (Fixed Index Annuity) represents the better upside growth potential.

In my opinion, these products are the best of the best income-producing annuities you can own in retirement. Millions of consumers agree, as indicated by the fact that FIAs have become the top-selling annuities in the marketplace today. Why are FIAs better than other types of annuities, in my opinion?

Fixed Index Annuity vs. Variable Annuity

I believe that principal protection is superior to market risk. Thus, I am not a fan of Variable Annuities (VAs). In my opinion, VAs are a waste of time and money. Clients who buy them are generally told, "They provide protection while offering unlimited growth at the same time." This is a half-truth. It exemplifies how something that sounds too good to be true, probably is! In truth, there is **no principal protection** of any kind in any VA. This is why they are called *variable* annuities. What varies? Your principal! Your principal value can go up or down. You can lose some or all of your principal in a VA, because an income rider in a VA only offers **income protection**, and it is offered at an additional fee. This income rider is also called a "living benefit." Of course, this sounds better than a dead benefit. Who wants a dead benefit? But the nomenclature can be misleading. A living benefit means that *it will not transfer to your beneficiaries at death*. A living benefit exists for the owner, only while the owner is among the living! When the owner dies, the living benefit stops. Only the *variable* account value will be passed on to beneficiaries.

The owner of the VA must sometimes pay an additional fee to include a spouse in the living benefit. That way, the income for the spouse is insured at the death of the VA's owner.

Why do I not like variable annuities? For me, it doesn't make sense to pay an average of 3.5% in fees to get lifetime income protection in a VA when lifetime income protection is available with *zero to 1% fees* in a Fixed Index Annuity (FIA). Why pay 3.5% in fees for the opportunity for unlimited growth? If growth is the goal, why not simply invest in a traditional growth portfolio at a fraction of the cost?

Variable Annuities also come with significant restrictions on the sub-accounts available on the risk side of the investment product. Why limit sub-accounts (what you can invest in) if higher growth is the goal?

Don't get seduced by the idea that you can have the best of both worlds. You can't. What you will likely end up owning in a Variable Annuity is the mediocre average of both worlds—at twice the cost! This means your financial adviser will often make twice as much for giving you less performance on both sides of the equation.

Advisers who want to sell VAs must possess both an *insurance license* and a *securities license*. Safe money advisors like myself only offer guaranteed insurance products, and thus we only need an insurance license. Because of this, many of my friends on the securities side of financial planning criticize my safe money advice to their clients: "Well, he doesn't have a securities license. Of course he's going to recommend an insurance product. What else can he do? He's *only* got a license to sell and recommend insurance products." I find the statement "He's *only*" quite offensive. It infers that an insurance license is somehow a lower-level license, and that an "insurance only" licensed financial adviser lacks the sophistication and intelligence to offer competent financial income planning advice. For the record, let me be clear. Sophistication and intelligence have *nothing* to do with why most safe money financial advisers (like myself) choose not to carry a securities license. Many of us actually have carried a securities license at some previous point in our career. When I began my career in the financial services industry, I acquired an insurance license *and a securities license*. Later, I made a conscious choice to lay aside my securities license. For personal reasons, making money off of other people's assumption of risk is just not appealing to me at this time in my professional life. A fixed-index annuity with principal protection and a guaranteed lifetime income account *ensures* my client's money will last and allows my client to be the one who benefits from it the longest. I believe this is what most people desire once they are retired.

Variable annuities are a fool's bet, in my opinion. According to an article published by the financial magazine *Barron's*, VAs carry one of the highest average fees (3.50%) of any financial product available today.[46] As of this writing

---

46 Karen Hube, "Top 50 Annuities," May 27, 2013. Accessed May 15, 2018 at https://www.barrons.com/articles/SB50001424052748704895304578495341390213604.

(January 2018), since the year 2000 the S&P 500 indices (with dividends re-invested) has averaged only about 5.5%.[47] To have earned a net return of 5.5% over that period of time in a VA, one would have had to achieve a gross return of 9.0%. I know of no VA that has matched such a difficult financial benchmark as the S&P 500 over this period of time, let alone beaten it! Even if one had simply matched the S&P 500, the net return after a 3.50% fee would have yielded only 2% to one's principal. With such high fees, many VAs may have actually realized a negative net (after-fee) return since the year 2000. Again, if not limiting growth is the goal, why not invest in a traditional growth equities account at a fraction of the cost?

Why any responsible financial adviser would recommend such a terrible "risk to reward" instrument as a VA today is baffling. Except, of course, that VAs are the highest compensated financial product ever produced by the world of Wall Street! That makes them the tool of choice for many Wall Street securities licensed advisers when clients express concern about the risk equities carry, especially as they head into their retirement years.

Many VAs are so complicated that even the professional selling them does not fully understand the details of what the client is promised. One thing is clear: no VA promises principal protection (wealth preservation). Only *income protection* is offered, and not always to both spouses. Who wants to pay a high fee for "protection" and then not have it protect their spouse once they are gone?

Fixed Index Annuities – Lowest Cost Lifetime Income Protection

Fixed Index Annuities (FIAs) offer 100% protection of principal from market risk, as well as both a single and joint lifetime income optional benefit. At the time of writing, some FIAs include a lifetime income account option benefit

---

47 DQYDJ, "S&P 500 Return Calculator, with Dividend Reinvestment," May 6, 2018. Accessed May 15, 2018 at https://dqydj.com/sp-500-return-calculator/.

without an additional fee. Others charge a small fee (approximately 1%) for the optional guaranteed lifetime income withdrawal benefit. These fees typically come with a guaranteed income account growth factor each year. Today, many of these guaranteed annual growth rate factors range from 5% to as high as 8%. Imagine the benefit of riding the final five or ten years of your working career with an IRA rolled over into an FIA that guarantees this kind of growth while eliminating all principal loss from market risk!

All FIAs are backed by the claims-paying ability of a life insurance company. The life insurance company gives a contractual guarantee that protects all invested principal from exposure to loss from market risk. The interest credited in a Fixed Index Annuity is tied to a benchmark market index such as the S&P 500, the Dow 30, the NASDAQ, etc. The better the index performs, the more potential interest that can be credited up to a maximum amount each crediting period. This "maximum" is often referred to as the "Cap." However, no principal is ever invested directly into these composite market indices. Consequently, when the index of choice experiences a negative loss, **the owner of a Fixed Index Annuity does not experience a loss of principal**. Owners of a Fixed Index Annuity can **only participate in the *gain* of an index**. They can **never participate in an index *loss***. This concept is illustrated in the graphic below:

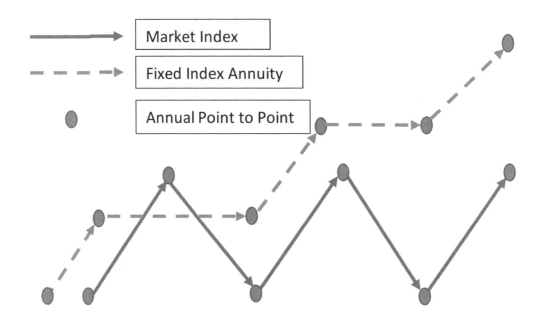

As illustrated, all market risk is eliminated. The absolute worst year possible in an FIA is a year of *zero interest*. During years of market loss, an FIA stays stable: no gain, no loss. Zero negative change due to market losses. When the market plummets, zero is a hero! You don't feel so bad about gaining zero when all your friends in the market lost money. When you purchase an FIA, you will never lose money due to market risk. Never!

In exchange for the elimination of all market risk, an FIA has three major conditions one must understand and accept.

FIA Condition Number One

As mentioned previously, the first condition is called a *cap*. A cap is simply the maximum amount of interest you can receive in a given contract period, usually one year on a point-to-point basis beginning with your policy effective date (e.g., June 5 of one year to June 5 the following year). The point is that, with a cap, *you may not get all of the index gains during a given period of time*. If the market shoots up 30%, you will not make 30% because your cap will be lower.

Insurance companies have multiple ways of "capping" interest potential in these products. The purpose of this book is not to "go into the weeds" concerning the intricacies of how each product is constructed (sorry, all you engineers). Our purpose here is only to make you aware of the three major conditions that govern all FIAs from a broad general perspective. You should consult your licensed professional to understand the details of each individual product.

FIA Condition Number Two

The second major condition is the *surrender period*. This is the length of time you must retain funds in the contract. You pledge not to end the contract for a set period of time known as "the surrender period," usually 3–16 years. A majority of the most popular FIAs today fall into a ten-year surrender period. This means you commit to keep at least a portion of your money in the FIA during the surrender period. However, during the surrender period, most FIAs allow you to withdraw 5% to 10% of the contract value or initial premium paid, annually without any penalty. Thus, you still have reasonable liquidity for income purposes during the surrender period. Unlike a traditional bank CD, FIAs offer substantial income liquidity during their "term" and were designed for individuals who wanted to preserve principal while still drawing an income from that principal without penalty. Once the surrender period has expired, a client can withdrawal up to 100% of remaining principal (plus accrued interest) at any time and without a surrender penalty.

FIA Condition Number Three

The third major condition is *tax-deferred interest income growth*. In all annuities, principal grows on a tax-deferred basis, even if the source of the principal is not a tax-deferred IRA, 401k, etc. In other words, even non-qualified money will receive the benefit of tax-deferred growth. All interest accrued in a fixed index annuity is taxed as ordinary income upon withdrawal only.

FIA Benefits

What outstanding benefits do FIAs provide?

We've already mentioned **protection of principal**. In an FIA, one's money is preserved from all market risk, 100% guaranteed by the issuing life insurance company. You simply cannot lose money in an FIA due to market loss or volatility. While this is a tremendous benefit, there is another benefit that can be even more valuable—an **optional lifetime income and/or joint lifetime income withdrawal guarantee**. When activated, this benefit can guarantee that regardless of how long you and/or your spouse live, neither can ever outlive the income streaming from the annuity.

Think of this benefit like a pension or Social Security payout. This income is guaranteed to be there as long as you are there! However, unlike a pension or Social Security payment, when a spouse passes away, the surviving spouse's benefit is never reduced! In other words, there is no "survivorship penalty." Income payments will continue at the same level for the surviving spouse as long as that spouse is alive. This benefit is a favorite among FIA owners because it secures peace of mind. Both spouses are fully protected from income loss for their whole lives.

Here's another benefit. Many FIAs offer the **potential of increased income** throughout the lifetime income phase of the contract. At the time of writing, some offer this increasing income opportunity without any fees. Others may require a nominal fee for this feature. Regardless, this is a tremendous optional feature, considering that many people retiring today could spend almost as many years in retirement as they did in the workforce. Time is a great enemy of money. Over time, inflation erodes money's **purchasing power**. What costs you $1 today will cost more a decade down the road. (Remember penny candy? It's not around anymore … because of inflation.)

FIAs can protect the purchasing power of your income. Set up properly, the FIA could increase your income to offset inflation. And, you need never fear exhausting the source of your income over time!

In retirement, most people want to **turn their savings into supplemental income**. Why would anyone not want to do this with an FIA that not only *guarantees income* but also *guarantees increased income* with each passing year? A remarkable guaranteed benefit!

Nursing Confinement Care and Terminal Illness Benefits in an FIA

Estimates suggest that over 70% of all people turning 65 today will experience the need for nursing confinement medical care.[48] As long as at least $1 remains in the contract's cash value, many FIAs offer an income multiplier of 50%–100% for up to five years while such care is received during a qualified nursing confinement period. No medical exam is needed for this benefit! For example, an income of $20,000 (taken annually from the annuity's lifetime income account) could be increased to $30,000 or even $40,000 for up to five years. Once the five-year period has been exhausted, or earlier if the client is no longer in a confined care situation, the income reverts back to the original amount. This is yet another benefit not offered in a bank CD or market-based brokerage IRA investment account. Insurance companies have attempted to engineer FIAs to cover a variety of concerns and scenarios people will likely face during their retirement years. This makes FIAs an outstanding and highly versatile retirement income product.

Retain 100% Control of Your Money

One final benefit we need to discuss is the death benefit and control of the cash value contained within the account. Many people have been terribly misled about what happens to their money once they have invested into a life insurance company and purchased an FIA. Many people commonly think they have forever given up future control of their cash. **This is simply not true.** In fact, the exact opposite is true. By protecting one's cash from market downturns, one has actually **increased control** over that cash—by not losing it! After all, how much control does one have over lost cash?

---

48 U.S. Department of Health and Human Services, "How Much Care Will You Need?" Accessed May 15, 2018 at https://longtermcare.acl.gov/the-basics/how-much-care-will-you-need.html.

Okay. But what about the cash in the FIA? Well, should one reach a place in life where the need for immediate cash exceeds the need for lifetime income, a policy owner can surrender part or all of the remaining cash value, take their cash balance, and go to Vegas (or do whatever else they want). In a FIA, if the owner passes away, the insurance company does not keep the balance left in the account. All remaining cash is passed on as a death benefit to the policy's named beneficiaries. The full 100% of the cash surrender value account value will go to a spouse or another beneficiary. Now that's control of one's money!

To find out more about how a Fixed Index Annuity and/or Investment Grade Life Insurance might fit into your overall retirement strategy, contact the financial professional who recommended this book to you. You can also receive additional information and copies of this book by visiting my website at www.worthlessira.com.

I can promise you one thing for certain: the market will not be the same tomorrow as it is today. But your retirement income doesn't have to change with the fortunes and perils of the market. You can guarantee your financial future. You can guarantee that neither you nor your spouse will ever see a day without the retirement income you have earned from a lifetime of hard work, sacrifice, and saving.

Income vs. no income—this is the difference between winning and losing in retirement.

Why not take the guaranteed win? Act now and avoid The Worth*less* IRA!

Have a peace-filled, successful retirement. Enjoy your money and your retirement!

Made in the USA
Middletown, DE
26 March 2021